BEATING

BURNOUT

AT WORK

PAULA DAVIS, JD, MAPP

BEATING

BURNOUT

AT WORK

WHY TEAMS HOLD
THE SECRET TO WELL-BEING
AND RESILIENCE

WHARTON
SCHOOL
PRESS
Philadelphia

© 2021 by Paula Davis

Published by Wharton School Press
The Wharton School
University of Pennsylvania
3620 Locust Walk
300 Steinberg Hall-Dietrich Hall
Philadelphia, PA 19104
Email: whartonschoolpress@wharton.upenn.edu
Website: wsp.wharton.upenn.edu

Ebook ISBN: 978-1-61363-111-9
Paperback ISBN: 978-1-61363-112-6

To my Grandpa Davis, and his best friend, Ray

Contents

Introduction

Why did you decide to leave your law practice? How did you have the courage to change careers? You did *what*? These are the questions I am most frequently asked, and I always smile at them. I have been researching, teaching, and talking about burnout, resilience, and well-being for the last 10 years, but I didn't intend for that to be my career path. I burned out during what became the last year of my law practice. My decision to change careers turned out to be an easy one because I was on the verge of a breakdown.

My burnout story starts in 2008. If you met me then, you would have seen a successful lawyer, on top of her game, closing several complex multimillion dollar commercial real estate deals each month. You may have even thought, "She has it all." But here's what you would have missed. I was physically and emotionally exhausted, and it was a different kind of tired than I had ever experienced. Getting out of bed to go to work had become exceedingly difficult, if not emotionally painful. One day when I was walking my golden retriever, Sadie, I closed my eyes briefly, mindful of the warm sun on my face. I woke to a wet nose nudging my hand—I had fallen asleep standing on the side of the road, holding her leash. When I wasn't working, I neglected friendships in favor of bad reality television. Every work or life curveball, no matter how minor, became major. While I was driving to my parents' house one day, my mom called asking if I would stop at the grocery store on my way. I had a level-15 reaction to her very basic request. It alarmed her so much that she hugged me when I got the house and asked me if I was OK. That was not my personality, and it was a red flag.

I had also become very cynical, even by lawyer standards. Each morning, I would walk into work and dart directly into my office, hoping that the pressures of the day would stay away as long as possible. When my clients asked about a legal issue, outwardly I was very professional. But inwardly, I would roll my eyes and think, "Really? You can't handle this on your own?" "Didn't we already talk about this?" "Does the world really need another mini-mall?" My job as a commercial real estate lawyer was to help developers sort through legal issues so that they could build mini-malls—I had to be on board with the concept. Disconnecting from people was unusual for me, and I just wanted to be left alone.

Eventually, I started to feel ineffective. I never lost confidence in my ability to be a good lawyer, but I started to think, "Why bother?" and "Who cares?" In conversations with clients, my inner dialogue would be, "You're not going to listen to my advice anyway, so why are we having this conversation?" I also stopped seeing a clear path for myself through the legal profession. I worked at a large law firm and then in-house in a corporate legal department. I had checked the progression boxes that other people told me mattered in my career, and it wasn't enough.

My burnout was severe, but it didn't start that way. It was a slow burn. I started going into work later most days, just an extra 10 minutes so that nobody would notice. Over time, I stopped having as many lunches, coffees, and conversations with my business clients and colleagues. When burnout progresses, it can feel as though you're trapped inside a box. I tried several ways to escape. My boss, Steve, actually cared; I told him how I felt. I didn't give him the whole story, I just told him that I wanted to work on other types of projects in the legal department. I positioned it as "good for my career to get more expertise in other areas." He was OK with having me do fewer real estate deals, but senior leadership was not. I also thought very seriously about going back to the law firm where I used to work. Had it not been for a #MeToo moment I experienced right before my departure, I probably would have returned to work there.

I didn't want to start over at another firm, so I decided to start my own business. My parents owned a business for 15 years, and I grew up in an entrepreneurial world. I knew that business ownership would be in the cards for me at some point, though I thought it would be much later in life. I decided to start a bakery and was accepted to a pastry school in New York City. I spent hours dreaming about school, the recipes I would develop, and the certainty of an eventual James Beard Award. I even landed a short internship at a hip and trendy restaurant in San Francisco near where my brother lived, and I used a week of vacation to go there and work. I was so certain of my future that I gave Steve my notice before leaving for San Francisco.

Do you see where this is going? I knew within hours of starting the internship that I had made a mistake. Working in a restaurant is grueling work. The long hours, standing on your feet all day, producing the same desserts somebody else invented was not for me. It felt nothing like the dream I had envisioned. But I had a bigger problem: saving my job! I called Steve as soon as work ended and explained the situation. He was very understanding, excited to have me return to the job nobody knew I left. I wish everybody a boss like Steve.

Although I was thankful to still have a job, I was back at square one. My burnout worsened and along with it came high levels of anxiety. As a result, I started to get panic attacks that came weekly, sometimes daily. In addition, the high levels of stress caused such severe stomachaches that I ended up in the emergency room twice. I saw more than a half-dozen doctors. None of them mentioned burnout or work or even asked how I was doing generally in life. I was at a point where, if someone had asked me how I was doing, I would have burst into tears. This would have revealed the truth I had been keeping a secret because I didn't want to be perceived as a weak lawyer who couldn't hack it.

My last day practicing law was June 24, 2009. A few months before that, I stumbled on an article that described exactly how I felt.

Until that point, I had not really known what burnout was, how it started, or why it had crept up on me. At that moment, though, I knew studying it was my path forward.

Recovering from burnout, interviewing others about their burnout experiences, coaching clients, teaching and training thousands of people, and studying the evolving and increasingly pervasive research have informed what I know burnout to be and, importantly, how it is prevented.

My dedication to helping other people led me eventually to create the Stress & Resilience Institute, where we focus on building practical strategies for companies who want to lessen the effects of burnout on their employees and build a more resilient, thriving, and engaged workplace.

Burnout amid a "New Normal"

Workplaces have long been stressful, but COVID-19 has raised the stakes. The pace of the modern workplace has sped up, and the work itself has become more complex. It's difficult for any one person to have the skills and expertise needed to meet the number of challenges your business partners, patients, and clients want solved. In addition, parents are trying to balance homeschooling kids with working. Generally, people are coping with not being able to see friends and family (and worrying about their health and well-being), celebrate milestones, or even pause five minutes to come up for air.

Burnout has become one of the most talked-about workplace topics, and its impact is far-reaching. The already-present 24/7 pace of work, a pandemic, a movement for racial equality, record unemployment, and a contentious election have combined to create a tsunami of stress, much of it feeling as though it's outside of your control.

But there is help, and you don't have to go it alone.

Recently, I finished a workshop about burnout prevention and was taking questions from participants. One leader asked, "But, Paula, how do I get burned-out people on my team to just do their jobs?" He clearly had missed the point. Employees will remember, for years to come, the ways in which leaders and teams step up right now. They will remember how the boss treated them in 2020; how their team leader responded to the rambunctious toddler who "Zoom bombed" the meeting; whether employees were allowed generally to take flextime to care for a sick loved one; and how leaders and organizations worked with single parents to relax billable hours or other production metrics. And when employees have the opportunity to take their talents elsewhere, how they were treated will strongly influence whether they stay or go.

Maybe you're reading this book because you're experiencing burnout, or because you're a leader who has seen burnout in your organization. My hope is that this book becomes a trusted resource and guide for busy professionals so that they have a better understanding of what burnout is and what causes it, and for organizations who are looking to help build and develop teams and leaders who thrive in a resilient way to prevent burnout.

Four Key Takeaways

As you read this book, there are a few important insights to keep in mind.

1. Burnout Is Complex

Preventing burnout requires a shift from a symptoms-only approach to a causes-also approach. Burnout is complex.[1] The self-help world tends to oversimplify burnout by focusing on the main symptom of it—exhaustion—and suggesting individual-based fixes such as yoga and meditation. You can do yoga and meditate to get a handle on certain types of stress, but you can't yoga or meditate your way out of burnout. Why? Because burnout is caused by factors that yoga and meditation can't fix, and most programs address the symptoms only, not the causes of burnout.

2. The Solution Is Systems Based

Preventing burnout requires a shift from individual-only strategies and programs to systems-based, holistic tools and frameworks focused at every level of the organization.

3. It's All About Teams

The best place to deploy these system-wide, holistic tools is within all the mini-systems that already exist in companies: their teams. Why? Most work is actually teamwork: 83% of workers say they do most of their work in teams.[2] And teams include individual performers and leaders, each of whom have an important role to play in this process. Teams that are resilient and thriving influence how engaged, creative, and innovative its members are.[3]

4. Tiny Noticeable Things Can Lead to Change

Even though burnout is complex, the tools and frameworks individuals, teams, and leaders need to prevent it are not. Most of them are tiny noticeable things (TNTs). Although easy, they still must be practiced. They may even require tweaks to the way you lead, think, or what you prioritize. But the payoff in terms of burnout prevention is significant.

How to Read This Book

In the following nine chapters, I offer the strategies and tools that most frequently resonate with the individuals, teams, and leaders that I teach and coach. The intent is not for you to use all these tools, but to identify the ones your team most needs. I take a science-help approach because I work with diverse organizations in healthcare, law, technology, and the military, and with busy professionals who want evidence-based insights.

Remember there is no one-size-fits-all approach to burnout prevention—each team's needs are different. I've worked with big, established tech firms such as Intel, the US Department of Defense, the US Army, and some of the world's largest law firms, and the burnout fix varies from team to team, organization to organization, and industry to industry.

Part I helps establish an understanding of what burnout is and how it can be addressed. Chapter 1 explains the burnout basics, providing a definition of burnout, an explanation of its causes, and a list of key warning signs. The specific factors that cause burnout are explained, along with the business case for investing in burnout prevention at work.

Chapter 2 explores the importance of looking at burnout holistically. It introduces two case studies—one from the Mayo Clinic and the other from the US Army—to illustrate how holistic-focused programs to prevent burnout and build resilience can succeed. Chapter 3 focuses specifically on teams as the point within the system to best deploy burnout prevention tools and frameworks. The way in which teams handle stress influences burnout, well-being, and resilience. The goal for teams is to increase their capacity to thrive and be resilient.[4] What emerges are a specific set of competencies that teams can develop, supported by specific tools and frameworks in intentionally targeted areas. The rest of the chapters explain these tools and frameworks in more detail. Chapter 3 introduces the PRIMED model, which will present the basis for leading your team to become more resilient.

Part II looks at the PRIMED model in detail. Chapter 4 explains the foundation needed to support thriving and resilient teams, which consists of psychological safety and psychological needs. People need to feel like they belong while at work and on their teams, have a say in how they work, and feel that they are developing as professionals. Chapter 5 goes into more detail about connection. High-quality relationships are central to resilience, thriving, happiness, and well-being. This chapter addresses the impact loneliness has, ways to keep your virtual team connected, the importance of capitalizing on good news, and it provides a framework for communicating about stress and burnout.

Chapter 6 is about impact: People need to know that their work contributes to something greater. Meaning, the 20% rule, connecting to your end user, and creating a supportive leadership style are discussed. Chapter 7 explores the importance of mental strength. A team's collective efficacy—the belief in their collective ability to overcome challenges and reach tough goals—is predictive of team resilience, engagement, and thriving.[5] The chapter discusses other ways individuals, leaders, and teams can increase their mental strength. Chapter 8 explores the importance of energy and stress awareness. Leaders can positively impact team stress and decrease burnout by focusing on five key strategies, while recognizing ways to mitigate the leader-producer dilemma. Also discussed is the importance of small wins as energy boosters, along with ways to identify icebergs or rules—specific core values and beliefs that can interfere with your ability to manage stress. The chapter concludes by suggesting ways to recover from burnout.

Finally, chapter 9 explores how thriving and resilient teams create cultures of continuous improvement and positive change to address aspects of team culture that must be tweaked. Appreciative inquiry, job crafting by identifying key resources, and developing design thinking mindsets are three processes teams (and individuals) can use to create continuous improvement and positive change.

PART I

Understanding the Problem

Chapter 1

Stress and Work in the Twenty-First Century
The Burnout Epidemic

$\mathbf{M}$eet Catherine.[1] I interviewed her several years ago in an ongoing effort to collect stories from busy professionals who were in the middle of burnout or had experienced it at some point in their careers. Catherine was in the same role for 12 years, working in a large hospital system. As is typical of most professionals I talk to, she wore many hats and served many people. She talked about how the competing demands and lack of communication on her team and within the organization as a whole made her job especially difficult. Her role eventually evolved into something more managerial: She was asked to spend more time focusing on strategy planning and people development, even though she was still asked to produce work associated with her prior job category.

Lack of communication, unclear expectations, the need to lead while still producing high-quality work, and stress generally took their toll. Although Catherine took pride early on in her career at reacting swiftly under pressure, now even the smallest stressors wore on her. She reported frequently clenching her fists, grinding her teeth, fatigue, and sleeplessness. Catherine scheduled a checkup with her primary care provider, thinking she had rheumatoid arthritis, but tests ruled it out.

Her doctor knew where she worked and told her that her symptoms were stress related. She told me she was at first offended, thinking she could "handle" whatever life threw at her. Then she broke down and cried.

Catherine's burnout story is not unusual. I have coached, taught, and interviewed thousands of people about burnout prevention, and my goal with this chapter is to invite you inside the world of burnout. The more you know about its causes, the three dimensions, and key warning signs, the earlier you can assess for yourself whether what you're experiencing is just stress or something more.

Working in a "VUCA World" Means Stress

VUCA is a military term that stands for volatile, uncertain, complex, and ambiguous. Researchers and professionals are starting to use it in the workplace generally to describe the stress associated with work. Teams face frequent change, increased workload, fewer resources, and more demanding customers and clients. Organizations, even whole industries, are changing and being hit constantly with increased regulations, technology, and competition.

Organizationally, leaders are managing globalization and increased regulation as the pace of work increases. In early 2020 the COVID-19 pandemic swept across the world, introducing new and unknown stressors to the world of work. Busy professionals were thrust into balancing work and life demands in a new way by trying to work and homeschool kids at the same time. The 24/7 "always on" pace accelerated, boundaries blurred, and always being at home made it nearly impossible to fully detach from work. And the movement for racial equality revealed that underrepresented groups have exhausted themselves trying to fit into organizations that continue to undersupport them.

It's no wonder, then, why burnout rates are high. Some recent research shows the breadth of the problem (and these statistics are pre-COVID-19):

- Up to 50% of physicians are experiencing burnout.[2]
- 96% of senior leaders report feeling burned out to some degree; one-third describe their burnout as extreme.[3]

- A workplace app for technology professionals includes a question about burnout: "Are you currently suffering from job burnout?" More than 57% of respondents said yes.[4]
- A survey of teachers found that 87% of respondents said the demands of their job are at least sometimes interfering with their family life. More than half reported that they don't have enough autonomy to do their job effectively, and only 14% said they felt respected by their administration. Both of these factors drive burnout.[5]
- In finance, 60% to 65% of bankers age 25 to 44 reported some level of burnout.[6]
- The Special Victim's Counsel in the US Air Force reported a burnout rate of 50%.[7]
- In one of the only empirical studies to measure burnout rates among lawyers, results showed that more than one-third of the lawyers scored above the 75th percentile on the burnout measure.[8]

Chronic stress is linked to higher rates of errors, safety issues, lack of concentration, lack of focus, and working memory problems, among other things. For many professionals, these are critical tools, and rates of errors and safety issues impact numerous industries where precision is critical.[9]

Physicians with burnout are twice as likely to be involved in patient safety incidents, twice as likely to have low patient satisfaction scores (the cynicism dimension of burnout alone more than quadrupled the odds of low patient-reported satisfaction), and twice as likely to exhibit low professionalism (e.g., low-quality communication and lack of empathy).[10] In another study, each *one point* increase in a surgeon's exhaustion and cynicism scores resulted in a 5% to 11% higher likelihood of reporting a medical error in the past three months.[11] That last finding underscores the fact that small shifts in burnout rates can dramatically impact others' health and safety.

One legal malpractice insurance carrier reported that the percentage of claims that had lawyer-related mistakes associated with them jumped from about 15% of total claims in 2012 to 63% of total claims in 2017.[12] As a result, claims attorneys at this insurance carrier interviewed their member general counsels to investigate the root causes of the increase. These were the most frequent responses received: the increased pace, the "always on," 24/7 nature of the practice, the increased complexity and specialization of practice areas, and the decrease in mentoring and personal interaction.

What Is Burnout?

The World Health Organization (WHO) updated its definition of burnout as a "syndrome conceptualized as resulting from chronic workplace stress that has not been successfully managed. It is characterized by three dimensions: (1) feelings of energy depletion or exhaustion; (2) increased mental distance from one's job, or feelings of negativism or cynicism related to one's job; and (3) reduced professional efficacy. Burnout refers specifically to phenomena in the occupational context and should not be applied to describe experiences in other areas of life."[13] The last sentence is an important one. The word "burnout" is often used synonymously with "stress" and therefore is applied generally and to a broad range of stressors. But, for our purposes, burnout is specifically a work-related issue.

The three big dimensions, or symptoms, of burnout are embedded within the WHO's definition, and it's important to distinguish them. Burnout is more than feeling tired because you're working on a big project or because you're in middle of your busy season (e.g., accountants during tax time). The dimensions of burnout are experienced chronically—more often than not over a period of time:[14]

- **Exhaustion**: This happens when you are physically and emotionally drained. Eventually, chronic exhaustion leads people to disconnect or distance themselves emotionally and cognitively from their work, likely as a way to cope with the overload.

- **Cynicism**: Everyone, from colleagues to clients to patients, starts to bother you. You start to distance yourself from these people by actively ignoring the qualities that make them unique and engaging, and the result is less empathy.
- **Inefficacy**: This is the "why bother, who cares" mentality that appears as you struggle to identify important resources and as it becomes more difficult to feel a sense of accomplishment and impact in your work.

These three symptoms of burnout can be measured, and my work with teams often starts there. The Maslach Burnout Inventory—General Survey—is the gold standard burnout measurement tool that measures each of the three symptoms.[15] It's important for me to understand the ways in which team members are feeling the effects of burnout and the impact burnout rates have on the team as a whole. Here is what I discovered after assessing burnout on a 19-person ophthalmology team at a children's hospital: Nine team members scored in the high category for exhaustion, and eight scored in the high category of cynicism. This team reported the highest scores in these categories that I have seen to date; some of the respondents had "perfect" scores. In this case, "perfect" isn't good; it means they answered "every day" (the highest score of six) to every question asking about how often they felt exhausted and cynical. Interestingly, eight team members scored in the low category for exhaustion, and nine team members scored in the low category for cynicism. The remaining team members were somewhere in the middle. This was truly an all-or-nothing team with burnout. The one thing that kept the team from going down in flames was its inordinately high scores on professional efficacy. Sixteen team members scored in the high category of professional efficacy, meaning that they knew their mission, knew they were good at their jobs, could effectively solve problems, and knew they were having a positive impact on the organization as a whole. A consistent extreme high workload over time and organizational politics and red tape were crushing their ability to thrive.

What Causes Burnout?

Burnout is caused by an imbalance between your job demands and job resources, and it's more likely to occur when job demands outweigh job resources.[16] **Job demands** are aspects of your work that require sustained effort and energy. **Job resources** are aspects of your work that give you motivation and energy and stimulate personal growth, learning, and development.[17] Table 1.1 provides examples of different job demands that influence burnout and job resources that promote well-being.[18]

Four of the job resources shown in table 1.1—autonomy and job control, development opportunities, role clarity, and participation in decision-making—appear to be the central resources for creating well-being and healthy workplaces.[19] Organizations that do not

Table 1.1. Job Demands and Resources

Job demands: The Core 6	Job resources
Lack of autonomy	High-quality relationships with colleagues; social support
High workload and work pressure, particularly without adequate staffing	Decision authority; participation in decision-making
Lack of support from leaders and/or colleagues	Feedback
Unfairness (lack of transparency; arbitrary decision-making; favoritism)	Autonomy and job control
Values disconnect	Development opportunities
Lack of recognition	Leader support
	Recognition
	Having meaningful work; impact
	Role clarity

prioritize these four enough may not be able to increase well-being effectively. Job resources not only help you achieve work goals and learn and grow at work but also help fulfill psychological needs, which are a foundational aspect of thriving and resilient teams (discussed in more detail in chapter 4). Job resources have been shown to predict dedication, workplace commitment, and turnover intention.[20]

Other job demands include emotionally demanding interactions with clients, colleagues, and patients, time pressure and encroachment on personal time, and lack of clarity about project direction and role fulfillment. Three of the Core 6 job demands—workload, having low autonomy or control over your job or job environment, and low social support at work—are among the top 10 most prominent workplace exposures that affect human health and longevity.[21] In addition, these workplace stressors have similar health impacts (i.e., poor physical health, poor mental health, morbidity, and mortality) as exposure to secondhand smoke.[22]

Importantly, many of the job demands listed above can be measured. The Core 6, in particular, can be evaluated with the Areas of Worklife Survey (AWS).[23] Once I know some of the specific causes of burnout for a team, then I tailor strategies and my conversations with leadership to address those causes. For example, I asked senior members of a marketing team at a medical device organization to take the AWS, which showed that workload and lack of recognition were two primary causes of burnout. Further coaching with some of the team revealed that lack of recognition meant not having a "seat at the table" in key meetings or not having a title they felt was commensurate with their work in the organization. Those were things senior leadership could fix. Workload issues are more difficult to remedy, especially during COVID-19, but they can and should be addressed.

You should be mindful of the relationship between burnout and engagement. Although engagement tools and frameworks have many benefits, recent research shows that engagement may occur in combination with burnout.[24] Workers classified as engaged-exhausted showed the highest turnover intention of any group in one study, even higher than those who were most burned out. For this group (representing almost 20% of the study participants), engagement was not a purely beneficial experience. The engaged-exhausted group had strong mixed feelings about their work. They reported high levels of interest in their work but also high levels of stress, often due to not having enough resources. The marketing team mentioned earlier was also in the top tier for engagement scores in their organization, yet nearly one-half of the team was burned out (having both high exhaustion and cynicism scores).

It's impossible to capture all the additional, industry-specific job demands in this book. For example, a big job demand for healthcare providers is note-taking in electronic health records; for lawyers it's tracking billable hours. What job demands are specific to your industry?

What Does Burnout Look and Feel Like?

Burnout is a manifestation of chronic workplace stress, but I think of it as a "gateway process," because it may open the door to other mental health issues, such as depression, anxiety, panic attacks, and other physical, psychological, emotional, and behavioral concerns.

In my personal and professional experience the worse burnout gets and the longer it lasts, the more likely you are to see more significant physical, psychological, and behavioral issues emerge. I experienced anxiety but not depression. For others, it's the opposite. For some, none of the above.

Here are some of the warning signs of burnout:[25]

- **Physical**: Frequent headaches, getting sick more often than usual, prolonged fatigue, stomach and digestive issues, restlessness, insomnia, heart palpitations, chest pain, cardiovascular disease, changes in pain experiences
- **Psychological**: Panic attacks, increasing feelings of anger, frustration and irritability, feeling hopeless, helpless, and pessimistic, loss of enjoyment for activities you once loved, depression, anxiety

- **Behavioral:** Drop in productivity, increased absenteeism, isolation—wanting to eat lunch alone or just be alone, coming into work later than usual on a more consistent basis, becoming a poor team player, mood changes, irritability, job dissatisfaction, increased alcohol/drug use

Most of these warning signs don't just happen overnight. I didn't suddenly get panic attacks and stomachaches. Those things manifested over a period of many months. If you can recognize the warning signs earlier, you may be able to stop burnout from accelerating.

Leaders also need to be educated about burnout, its causes, and its symptoms.[26] Leaders may unintentionally make burnout worse by dismissing it or thinking it's the same thing as general stress. Telling people to "take Friday off" or "take a vacation" will not alleviate burnout. Research shows burnout rates do decline during and immediately after vacation but return to prevacation levels within weeks.[27] One of my coaching clients actually savored her early COVID-19 "quarantine." She's recovering from a pretty severe case of burnout, and being able to stay home and not go into work helped her recovery.

The Business Case for Preventing Burnout

Burnout affects organizational well-being too. Burnout is closely linked to the following:

- Rates of errors[28]
- Turnover[29]
- Absenteeism[30]
- Decreased productivity[31]
- Quality, safety, and patient/client satisfaction[32]

Everything on this list has a quantifiable impact to your organization's bottom line. One healthcare industry study found that physicians who experienced burnout at one point in time had 168%

higher odds of leaving the organization two years later compared to those who did not experience burnout. Those who reported an intent to leave were three times as likely to have left.[33]

This is a simple calculation you can use: Turnover costs equal the number of employees you have, times the rate of attrition in your organization or industry, times the cost to replace someone (usually estimated at about 1.5 to 2 times salary).

If the skills, tools, and frameworks found in this book can reduce burnout by even a fraction of the current rate, organizations will be able to save millions of dollars.

Burnout Basics: Things to Remember

- Burnout is the manifestation of chronic workplace stress.
- The three main symptoms of burnout are chronic exhaustion, cynicism, and inefficacy.
- Burnout is caused by an imbalance between certain job demands and job resources.
- Leaders need to understand burnout so that they don't minimize it or inadvertently make it worse.
- Burnout hurts organizations, too, and impacts their financial health and well-being.

Chapter 2

Taking a Holistic Approach to Burnout Prevention and Well-Being at Work

Taking a holistic approach to burnout prevention might be a new way to think for your organization. Luckily, workplaces can follow the lead of the Mayo Clinic and the US Army, each of which took a different approach to tackling burnout prevention, resilience, and well-being at work.

The Mayo Clinic (Mayo) is an American academic medical center based in Rochester, Minnesota. Mayo has more than 4,000 physicians and scientists on staff with more than 61,000 employees overall and ranks near the top of all major published quality indexes with one of the lowest attrition rates in the country.[1]

In response to studies quantifying physician burnout, Mayo enacted a number of changes. In the two years following these changes, its physician burnout rate decreased by 7% despite an 11% rise in the rate of physician burnout nationally.[2] Importantly, the reduction was achieved while also reducing employee burnout generally and "despite having to implement a variety of other changes to improve efficiency, decrease costs, and increase productivity during the same interval."[3]

Central to Mayo's success in reducing burnout is its Listen-Act-Develop model—a research-based, integrated strategy designed to address the institutional drivers of burnout, foster resiliency, and sponsor physician leadership development.[4] The goals of the model are the following:[5]

- Prioritize employee's psychological needs of autonomy, social connection, and excellence (an important foundation of burnout prevention discussed in more detail in chapter 4)
- Facilitate teamwork
- Identify both institutional and local/unit drivers of burnout
- Design improved systems and processes
- Support the development of both physician leaders and good relationships between the organization and physicians

Table 2.1 lists ways Mayo has continued to operationalize the Listen-Act-Develop model.

Why a Holistic Approach Makes Sense

Organizational policies, decision-making, regulations, and more trickle down to influence the stress levels of teams, leaders, and frontline workers. Individual behaviors influence outcomes with clients, customers, and patients in a way that informs company policy and vice versa, and each industry is different.

Political, social, and economic issues shape your work environment in ways that promote stress.[6] The COVID-19 pandemic has

Table 2.1. Putting Listen-Act-Develop into Practice

Listen	Act	Develop
Identify and understand both the institutional and frontline drivers of burnout	Empower physicians to implement solutions to address the burnout drivers identified	Select and develop physician leaders
Create focus groups to discuss the main burnout drivers	Give the physicians tools and adequate funding to make this happen	Support leadership development with coaching, mentoring, assessment, and stretch assignments
Create an actionable plan meant to focus on alleviating the drivers of greatest concern	Track and measure progress; refine process and procedures as necessary	Provide feedback to frontline leaders and resources to help them to continue to develop as a leader

upended every aspect of almost every industry and will reshape how people work going forward. And although research has consistently pointed to management and leadership practices and poor job design as leading causes of burnout,[7] the majority of programs used to prevent burnout at work are individual based. One study found that organizational-directed interventions were more likely to lead to reductions in burnout, with those programs that combined structural changes, fostering team communication, cultivating teamwork, and enhancing job control (autonomy) as the most effective.[8] Another study that reviewed more than 25 individual studies about the efficacy of burnout prevention programs found that the combination of programs directed at both individuals and organizations led to better results for burnout and mental health, and the effects of these programs were longer lasting than individual-directed programs alone.[9] A recent meta-analysis reviewing interventions to alleviate burnout reached the same conclusion—that studies on stress and burnout prevention have shown promising results when individual and occupational strategies have been combined.[10]

More problematic is that individual-directed programs alone can easily become "check the block" training. Many organizations develop these types of programs, roll them out, and then do not provide ongoing support for these programs. Organizations that become expert at implementing well-being initiatives have the following features:

- Shared accountability for well-being among organizational leaders who prioritize it
- System-level interventions that are measured
- Usage of design-thinking methodologies to redesign broken systems and aspects of culture
- Consideration of well-being as a strategic investment
- A clearly articulated business case for well-being
- Operational decisions that consider well-being[11]

I have seen firsthand how this process gets stalled in the legal profession. Studies showing poor lawyer mental health have been around since the late 1980s, but efforts to finally do something about the problem galvanized only in the past few years. The legal profession continues to increase the amount of time and money it devotes to mental health and well-being. The American Bar Association and many law firms have introduced well-being weeks, chair massages, meditation and yoga training, and a number of programs aimed at individuals. Yet, the *American Lawyer*'s latest mental health and substance abuse survey asked lawyers to identify the aspects of their job that negatively impact their mental health and well-being. The factors cited most frequently were the feeling of always being on-call, inability to disconnect, lack of sleep, client demands, and billable hours pressure.[12] In addition, 73% of the respondents answered affirmatively when asked whether their work environment contributes to mental health issues.[13] Do you see the disconnect? These are the same types of job demands my coaching clients explore with me when talking about stress and burnout. These deeper conversations about focusing at a holistic level are the ones legal organizations (and organizations generally) must start having to make meaningful change. The COVID-19 pandemic and the impact it has had on the working world may force this conversation, or organizations will continue to lose valuable talent.

Lessons Learned from the US Army

When I started my business, I wanted to be a pioneer. I wanted to be at the forefront of creating something entirely new and different. Luckily, I've had the opportunity to help lead change in two industries, and my first experience was with the military. Never did I think I would work with drill sergeants and soldiers in any capacity. The Comprehensive Soldier and Family Fitness (CSF2) program was created while I was still practicing law. The pilot took place as I was starting my positive psychology studies at the University of Pennsylvania. During our first week of classes, I was inspired when Dr. Martin Seligman talked about CSF2.

As my year progressed, I became deeply interested in the science of resilience. The Penn Resilience Program is one of the most studied resilience programs. It has been adapted and taught to military and healthcare professionals, first responders, athletes (collegiate and professional), educators, and via my own work in some of these industries and within the legal profession.[14] I graduated in August 2010 and was invited to apply to become part of the Penn-CSF2 training team, teaching resilience skills to soldiers and their families and training them how to use these skills. I was a member of the fourth Master Resilience Trainer (MRT) facilitator course held in October 2010. Making it that far did not guarantee that I would make the team; in fact, I had to turn in all my study materials and workbooks once the course ended. We were told we would be contacted at some point if we "passed," so I waited. I received good news: I was assigned to my first training in January 2011.

The CSF2 program is an integrated, proactive approach to developing resilience and well-being in soldiers, their family members, and the US Army's civilian workforce. Gen. George W. Casey Jr.'s vision was that "CSF2 becomes part of our culture over time, with our soldiers understanding the positive dimension of psychological fitness much like professional athletes do."[15] During my time working in this program, CSF2 consisted of four components:

- Online assessment tool for all soldiers, called the Global Assessment Tool (GAT), which was used to identify resilience strengths and areas of improvement
- Online self-help modules tailored to the GAT results
- MRT courses using a train-the-trainer method to teach senior officers and noncommissioned officers resilience tools and skills
- Mandatory resilience training at every US Army leader development school

The train-the-trainer aspect was critical because Gen. Casey didn't want to just train soldiers—he wanted those soldiers to go back to their units to teach other soldiers the same skills. In the months that followed, Dr. Seligman, Brigadier General Rhonda Cornum, Dr. Karen Reivich, and colleagues created the US Army's MRT curriculum. What began as a meeting in 2008 has resulted in the Penn-CSF2 team having trained almost 40,000 MRTs.[16]

Active MRTs conduct resilience training of small groups as a mandatory component of the US Army's basic training and leadership development programs. As CSF2 has evolved, it is now housed under the US Army's Ready and Resilient Campaign, a comprehensive plan that integrates resilience into US Army programs and assessment.[17]

What Mayo and the US Army Got Right

Incorporating systemic solutions to address burnout and build resilience takes time, but the US Army and Mayo cases point to specific behaviors within these organizations that set up each of their respective programs for success. The following are examples of what the US Army and Mayo got right.

Acknowledge and Assess the Problem

Both the US Army and Mayo were willing to look at the data and acknowledge that there was a problem that must be addressed. Soldiers were suffering from poor mental health as a result of years of ongoing deployments. Healthcare professionals, particularly physicians, have seen steady increases in burnout rates. Many organizations resist assessing the problem for many reasons. Some don't want to know the extent of the problem. Others worry they won't have the ability to fix the problems that are discovered.

Burnout exists in your organization whether you measure it or not. As with other health concerns, it's best to catch burnout as early as possible.

Leverage Leadership

In both organizations, leaders at the highest levels became involved early. I thought that if the chief of staff of the US Army directed something to happen, it just happened. I was wrong.

Gen. Casey and his leadership team made extensive efforts to inform leadership at all levels about the program, the research efficacy supporting it, its components, and the benefits. In 2014 Raymond F. Chandler III, Sergeant Major of the Army, along with US Army Chief of Staff Raymond T. Odierno and US Army Secretary John M. McHugh, executed what became known as the "tri-signed letter," a directive signed by the highest-ranking US Army officials calling on all US Army leaders to make resilience training a priority. Eventually, officials developed executive briefings, and MRT primary instructors were trained to deliver those briefings to leadership within their units. US Army leadership was strategic in selling the program to their colleagues, who could then influence others to embrace the change, rather than resist it or go about it half-heartedly.[18]

Mayo has taken additional steps to continue to assess leadership behaviors that affect burnout, and simple changes have big results. Mayo discovered that each one-point increase in a leader's composite leadership score was associated with a 3.3% decrease in burnout and a 9.0% increase in the likelihood of professional satisfaction in those they supervised.[19]

Use Science and Stories

Science and stories are two of the best ways to defeat skepticism. Mayo's Listen-Act-Develop model is informed by studies from organizational psychology, social science, and positive organizational psychology.[20]

Gen. Casey approached Dr. Seligman and his team at the University of Pennsylvania because it was one of the only known institutions that had conducted this type of large-scale training *and* had published extensive peer-reviewed research in the area. It was also the only known entity that had extensive experience developing and implementing a resilience train-the-trainer model that had also been scientifically reviewed.[21]

Holistic programs have the power to inspire and transform an entire organization and those who work in it, and stories of transformation make the work come to life and concepts stick. The last place I thought I would learn anything about vulnerability was from US Army drill sergeants. Yet I can speak personally about my own transformation working with them. I used to be someone who never talked about failure or my own challenges. It was too risky, especially when I was practicing law. But the soldiers helped me understand that talking about your obstacles isn't a sign of weakness—it's courageous and inspiring. Here are two examples.

One participant was a quiet soldier. During one of our breakout sessions, his hand shot up. "I'm an asshole!" he said. It took the room by surprise and, naturally, we asked him to explain. "I'm on my third marriage, and it isn't going well. I just now realized that I've been a big part of the problem!" Although there were a few chuckles, we all respected the profound moment of self-awareness.

Another soldier spoke about his experience at the Pentagon during the September 11, 2001, terrorist attack. He recounted the intense emotion he felt in the subsequent weeks and months, such that he eventually attempted to take his own life. He was found in his car by a relative and survived. He said, with tears streaming down his face, "If I had these skills earlier, I could have at least slowed down my anxiety and the emotion so that I could have gotten help."

These case studies illustrate that holistic change can be implemented in different ways to decrease burnout and increase resilience and well-being at work. However, for many organizations, figuring out the best starting place is hard (hence the tendency to lean on individual programs). The next chapter explains why workplace teams are uniquely suited to take up this challenge.

Burnout Basics: Things to Remember

- Burnout is a systemic problem that requires a holistic approach from organizations, meaning that organizations need to understand team, leader, and frontline worker stress and address it collectively.

- Organizations don't have to start at square one: Mayo and the US Army are two cases that leaders can learn from and incorporate into their organizations.
- Organizations need to acknowledge and assess the problem, leverage leadership, and use science-based methods in combination with stories that inspire and encourage.

Chapter 3

The Power of Teams to Help Your Organization Prevent Burnout

Teams are powerful entities within organizations and are under-utilized when it comes to burnout prevention.

Given the increased complexity of work and the rapid pace of change in many work environments (now amplified by the COVID-19 pandemic), professionals need to team up to effectively solve problems. Research shows that individuals are much more successful when working in teams.[1] In addition, COVID-19 has likely permanently changed how work will be done. It's realistic to assume that a hybrid in-person and virtual model of work will be the norm, where teams become even more important.

When I talked to Alyssa Brennan, Director of Strategic Initiatives at Google, Global Security and Resilience Services, she explained that our business environment is an artifact of an old system and old way of working.[2] "We built a nonterritorial, boundary-free space called 'the Cloud,' that has called into question our reliance on the physical boundaries of countries. Only teams can absorb this level of globalization," she said. She explained that the team she leads works on high-stakes security matters and they rely on each other to navigate complex challenges that are usually global in scope.

What Is a Team?

My favorite definition of "team" is two or more people who work together to accomplish shared goals. True teams are highly interdependent: They make plans, solve problems, and review progress, all in service of executing a common goal. The word "team" can be confusing to many professionals because they team (a verb). Teaming is the act of working with a few other people for a few weeks or months to complete a project. When the project is done, the team then disbands and reforms in new ways and with new people for different tasks. As a result, many professionals may be part of multiple teams during any given year.

Teaming takes practice. Even if you're teaming for only a few days or weeks, you need to be intentional about creating context, establishing specific goals, defining responsibilities, and talking about each other's working styles and strengths (and this is a two-way street between leaders and their direct reports).[3] Launching an effective teaming experience doesn't have to take much time. Taking 20 to 30 minutes at the beginning of a project to create an intentional start will save you more time during the project because you have established transparency, clarity, and norms. This is evident in healthcare teams, where medical personnel may have to become part of a new care team at each shift change and where team huddles— the quick moments team members come together to exchange important information and updates—help to facilitate frequent teaming.[4]

Importantly, teams that "team" well create a powerful learning environment, where it's expected that team members ask each other questions, share information, seek help, talk about mistakes, and get feedback.[5] In addition, research shows the ways in which teams manage stress influence burnout rates, well-being, and resilience:[6]

- High-quality teamwork is associated with well-being and resilience.[7]
- Working in a tight team structure and perceptions of greater team culture are associated with less exhaustion; stronger team culture is associated with less exhaustion among staff.[8]
- A person's perceived level of job control along with team efficacy mitigates key workplace stressors.[9]

- Team members' job demands positively predict both emotional exhaustion and burnout.[10]
- Work overload in military teams decreases their cohesion and leads to perceptions of inferior performance at both the individual and team levels.[11]
- The level or quality of teamwork partially explains the relationship between work demands and burnout.[12]
- There is a strong association among effective leadership, team behaviors, and job satisfaction.[13]
- A team-based training focused on building high-quality relationships and increasing social support, prioritizing feedback and communication, and addressing the perception of job resources lead to significantly less exhaustion (the lower levels were found even six months after the training stopped) and cynicism, two main symptoms of burnout.[14]

Teams Must Thrive and Be Resilient

Because teams are the key to burnout prevention at work, they need specific skills, tools, and frameworks to help them prevent it. Teams need to create cultures that will protect against the job demands that drive burnout and quickly pivot and adapt to shifting priorities, stress, setbacks, and change generally. And they have to do this while continuing to learn, grow, and stay motivated. Teams must be thriving and resilient.

Burnout is a manifestation of workplace stress, and resilience skills have proven to be effective in helping people better manage and grow from stress, challenge, and adversity.[15] Resilience is a skill set that activates the ability to navigate stress and change and to grow and thrive from challenges.[16] What's more encouraging is the body of research showing the importance of resilience at the team level and that groups can build resilience skills just like individuals. Resilient teams anticipate challenges, are aware of each other's capacity level, provide ongoing status updates to team members during a crisis, know when to go outside of the team for help, debrief regularly, and communicate appreciation.[17] Although resilience is a foundational ingredient of burnout prevention, thriving adds an important layer to the formula.

Thriving is a broader construct defined simply as a combination of vitality and learning and growth at work,[18] and it has been researched at the individual and team level.[19] Thriving teams are also resilient: They collectively view tough situations as challenges and opportunities and are energized by the challenge. There is a link between high-thriving teams and the ability to quickly respond to change in a positive way.[20] In addition, "thriving teams consist of individuals who are analytical, intrinsically motivated, learning-oriented and resilient, who come together with a diverse set of skills yet who still 'fit' together as a cohesive team. They are supported by (1) leaders who set vision and strategy and act as a coach/mentor and (2) organizational systems such as process, training and the resources and tools needed to do their jobs. These teams are surrounded by a culture that values continuous improvement, adaptation, and voice."[21] And most importantly for our purposes, there is a strong and negative correlation between thriving and burnout,[22] with thriving suggested as a framework to mitigate burnout.[23]

How to Build Thriving and Resilient Teams: The PRIMED Model

Thriving and resilient teams have a blend of characteristics that help them to be resilient and perform at their peak. These shared competencies include the following:[24]

- Psychological safety and trust; team members have autonomy support, feel like they belong, and continually learn and grow
- Structure and clarity with clear roles and goals that are specific, challenging, and attainable, supported by resources that are known to the group

- Prosocial interaction, social support, and high-quality connections supported by dependability, effective communication, and feedback
- Clear sources of meaning and impact that are discussed and values that are lived
- Good stress management routines and being alert to signs of overload in team members (with a willingness to do something about the sources of stress); understanding what builds and drains the team's energy
- Mental strength, including the shared belief in the team's ability to perform a task and overcome challenges and obstacles
- Supporting all this, the very best teams have a culture of continuous improvement and positive change—new ways of working when existing processes, values, and goals no longer serve them

These competencies can be distilled into the following six pathways you can remember with the acronym PRIMED:

- **Psychological safety and psychological needs**: Psychological safety and psychological needs are the important foundation of thriving and resilient teams. People need to feel like they belong while at work, enjoy some measure of autonomy, have the ability to create connection with others, and learn and grow as professionals.
- **Relationships**: High-quality relationships promote thriving and resilience.
- **Impact**: Thriving and resilient teams know that their work contributes to something greater and can see how it fits within the organizational system as a whole.
- **Mental strength**: A team's collective efficacy—the belief in their collective ability to overcome challenges and reach tough goals—is predictive of team resilience, engagement,

and thriving.[25] What teams think and how they think together are particularly important for teams that have to adapt to dynamic circumstances.[26]

- **Energy**: Building stress awareness helps teams preserve energy. Thriving and resilient teams do a good job of managing their stress and recognizing signs of stress and overload in each other.
- **Design**: Thriving and resilient teams create positive change when things aren't going right. Appreciative inquiry, prioritizing job resources, and cultivating a design mindset are three processes individuals and teams can use to create positive change.

Measuring Team Resilience

To better assess teams on these core competencies, I created a Resilient Teams Inventory that I use to help them pinpoint areas of team resilience that are working well or need to be improved. Table 3.1 includes some of the statements I use to evaluate team resilience. The scale for each question ranges from 1 to 5, with 1 being "strongly disagree" and 5 being "strongly agree." If you score between 41 and 50, your team is showing signs of resilience and thriving. If it is between 31 and 40, your team has some strengths, but it also has areas of improvement. Any lower than 30, and you have some serious work to do. Is your team PRIMED for resilience, thriving, and sustainable success?

The remaining chapters explain each pathway in the PRIMED model in more detail so that you, your team, and leaders have the tools and frameworks needed to build thriving and resilience and prevent burnout.

Table 3.1. Resilient Teams Inventory

Statement	Score
1. We know our resources and use them regularly.	
2. We adapt well to change.	
3. Setbacks don't affect our team for long—we pivot quickly.	
4. We pay attention and respond to early signs of stress and burnout in team members.	
5. Being on this team is energizing.	
6. Our work is a source of meaning and inspiration, and we regularly discuss the impact we make within the organization.	
7. We are good at having difficult conversations within the group.	
8. It's easy to ask other members of this team for help.	
9. We are focused on learning and growth and continually improving how our team works.	
10. My team members trust each other.	

Burnout Basics: Things to Remember

- Teams are a powerful place within your workplace system to address burnout. Teams are mini-systems or cultures that can successfully deploy the holistic strategies and frameworks shown to prevent burnout at work.
- The antidote to burnout is to create thriving and resilient teams, and these teams have seven core competencies operationalized as six different pathways. You can remember the pathways with the acronym PRIMED.

PART II

PRIMED for Team Success

Chapter 4

Psychological Safety and Psychological Needs
The Foundation

I t matters enormously to your well-being that you can show up as yourself to work and be seen. Knowing how to foster belonging and motivation will help your teams be more engaged, more committed to your organization, and more capable of managing the multitude of challenges they face. PRIMED teams need to prioritize two foundational building blocks: psychological safety and psychological needs—the "P" in the PRIMED model.

Foundation 1: Psychological Safety

I was co-teaching a workshop to a group of engineering executives about resilience when I realized I had been using a term, "ROI," without defining it. I asked if anyone was unfamiliar with the term. Sure enough, one person, who I'll call Sarah, raised her hand. She said, "I don't know what you mean." I explained that ROI meant "return on investment" and moved on with my presentation. Moments later, a different person in the back of the room, who I'll call Lisa, interrupted us and said in a loud voice, "I want to know who the person was who didn't know what ROI meant!" I was stunned. Everyone became silent, and Sarah was some combination of annoyed and embarrassed. To her credit, she outed herself.

What are the odds that Sarah will ever want to work with Lisa? Luckily, they are peers at the same level in their careers, but imagine for a moment that Sarah is Lisa's subordinate. How might Sarah feel each day at work, knowing that for some people, there is such a thing as a "stupid question"?

Psychological safety is the belief that you can be yourself, take good risks, ask questions, share partially formed ideas, raise problems, and respectfully disagree within your team without worry of being embarrassed, singled out, or penalized. It's trust at the team level.

The reason psychological safety is so important is that its benefits are significant, particularly in today's knowledge-based work environment. When team members feel psychologically safe, they feel comfortable speaking up and are more likely to identify serious issues or errors earlier, which could save lives or avert serious safety issues in some industries. They're also more likely to think creatively, share innovative ideas, and share their expertise. And, most importantly, psychological safety is the entry point for belonging, one of your core psychological needs I'll discuss later.[1] Belonging is also an important topic in diversity, equity, and inclusion conversations. Feeling like you don't belong or have to be someone different to fit in at work is exhausting. The movement for racial equality has made clear that the workplace must greatly improve in this area.

To feel this sense of belonging, to feel fully present and included at work, teams have to be able to have hard conversations and talk about failure. Teams that have cultivated a psychologically safe environment have members who don't have to put on a "work face" when they get to the office.[2]

Psychological safety and team performance go hand-in-hand. Google discovered this when it launched Project Aristotle, an initiative to study how to create high-performing and effective teams. After collecting the data, Google couldn't predict any sort of patterns about what made for a high-performing team until it factored psychological safety into the equation. Their research revealed that psychological safety, more than any other factor, was critical to making a team work.[3] Mary Shen O'Carroll, Google's Director of Legal Operations, and her team were part of the study. She told me that communicating consistently, being intentional about the way she shows up as a leader, and being transparent are the key leadership behaviors that help her team maintain psychological safety.[4]

Table 4.1 outlines other key behaviors that build psychological safety and the role you can play within your team to develop it.[5]

Table 4.1. How to Create Psychological Safety at Work

Leader behaviors that build psychological safety	Individual behaviors that build psychological safety
Be accessible and approachable; let team members know how and when it's best to reach you.	Maintain high-quality connections with team members.[6] People in high-quality relationships know that they are appreciated and valued, even if the interaction is short in duration. When people feel appreciated and valued, they are more likely to feel safe speaking up and discussing problems.
Increase attentiveness by acknowledging when someone has entered the room; look up from your phone/computer; close computer laptop.	Limit side conversations, cliques, and gossip.
Be clear about team standards and values and handle violations consistently.	Regularly deploy small attentive courtesies, such as looking someone in the eye when she speaks and saying thank you.
Give each person a say and seek out contributions and ideas (invite each team member to give both a pro and a con for an idea you're considering).	Offer peer-to-peer recognition; "catch" your colleagues doing something right.
Acknowledge the limits of your own knowledge; it's OK to say, "I don't know the answer" or "I've never seen this before."	Recognize when a team member needs help and reach out.
When a team member takes a well-intentioned risk that backfires, highlight it as a learning opportunity; go a step further and acknowledge times you've failed or fallen short.	Solicit input, feedback, and opinions from your teammates.
Provide transparency and ongoing status updates.	Offer encouragement to team members even if new ideas were not adopted.
Clarify roles and goals for teams that are now required to meet remotely; disruptive events may create new and competing tasks for teams.	
Rotate leadership of meetings.	

Cultural norms may impact how psychological safety is developed on teams, and all team members need to be aware of these cultural norms. One of my workshop participants appointed himself the "welcoming person" for new hires to educate them about cultural differences in his organization.

Foundation 2: Satisfaction of Psychological Needs

When I burned out, I would stay up late on Sunday night, staring at the clock, hoping to freeze time. I would have done anything to avoid going into work. One of my workshop participants called this feeling the "Sunday scaries." Teams can cultivate the motivation they need to prevent burnout by focusing on three important building blocks called "psychological needs": autonomy, belonging, and competence. These needs are essential nutrients for growth, high-quality performance, and well-being at work.[7] I will refer to them throughout the book as "your ABCs" or "ABC needs."[8]

My coaching client Julie captured the importance of ABC needs like this: Julie is a midlevel leader at a large professional services firm. She feels anxious taking an hour for herself or enjoying a date with her boyfriend because she's worried she will miss a critical client email or note from her boss. After we talked about the importance of ABC needs, she said, "Wow. If I had even 25% of this at work, I would totally leave my boyfriend!" I laughed, and then I asked her to explain. She said, "It would mean I would feel valued, so I would be happy to skip an occasional date night to handle an urgent work request."

The following is a little bit more detail about each ABC need.

Autonomy

You feel like you have some choice as to how and when you perform the various tasks that make up your job and how you execute your daily responsibilities. You have a say in the way things are done. And you can take initiative and make decisions about your work.

Autonomy does not mean going it alone or individualism. It is so powerful that one large study of physicians showed that having a low sense of autonomy in the practice environment was the single most powerful predictor of burnout.[9]

Lack of autonomy is a common theme in my coaching conversations. My coaching client Jen had a senior government position for more than 10 years. She had the freedom to come and go as she wished and was looped in on important decisions. As long as the work got done, she was pretty much left alone. She switched jobs and went into a more corporate role at a large organization and found it stressful to all of a sudden feel "checked up on." When I caught up with her almost a year after we initially talked, she had a bit of a different perspective and taught me an important lesson: Autonomy must be earned. There is no substitute for putting in time and doing good work. She had done that, and more autonomy followed.

Autonomy Quiz

This short quiz will quickly help you determine whether team members perceive autonomy at work. Ask them to take this quiz and answer each statement "yes" or "no."[10]

1. I feel like I have some choice in how I execute my day-to-day responsibilities.
2. I have a say in the way my day-to-day work gets done.
3. I am part of the decision-making process on changes that impact me and my work.
4. I have the necessary skills <u>and</u> support to improve my day-to-day work.

Once team members have taken the quiz, discuss any "no" responses.

Belonging

This is your desire to feel connected to others, to feel like you belong to groups that are important and significant to you, to feel cared for by others, and to value creating strong relationships.

Competence

You to feel like you're getting better at goals that matter to you. You feel effective in your work role. And you want to continue to grow and develop as a professional and master new skills.

Important workplace outcomes are associated with ABC needs satisfaction, including better job performance, decreased risk of burnout, stronger organizational commitment, and lower turnover.[11] ABC needs have been found to influence each of the three burnout components in various ways such that deprivation of any ABC need could lead to burnout.[12] In fact, satisfaction of each ABC component is negatively correlated with burnout.[13]

One of my coaching clients, Jill, is a senior leader in a large healthcare organization. Not having her competence need met was driving her burnout. She said all she wants at work is a seat at the table. She was frustrated when she received texts from her boss, who is present in these types of meetings, asking for her opinion on matters she could easily address if she were present.

Importantly, as your ABCs are met, peak performance becomes more likely. Your motivation improves and becomes more autonomous or high quality—meaning you are engaging in an activity because it's your choice and it aligns with your values. When your ABC needs are not met at work, you are more likely to be depressed, physically and emotionally exhausted, stressed, and have a higher turnover intention.[14]

What an ABC Culture Feels Like

It's easy to identify work cultures that promote ABC needs. I had the good fortune of working with a variety of teams at Defenders/ADT, experts in the home security industry. I talked to security advisers, security managers, sales professionals, and customer experience teams, but they taught me a lot about culture. They live by a set of passions and core values that guide everything about their organization. Although most organizations have core values or similar statements, at Defenders they actively promote ABC needs. The company emphasizes growth-oriented learning, helping their professionals expand their influence both at work and outside of work, and belonging. In fact, when I asked some of the learning and development team what kept them at the organization so long, themes of learning, growth, and relationships with others were critical.

For a different organization, I interviewed a group of leaders about what made them so happy at work (an "anti-burnout" interview of sorts). What one person said oozes ABC needs: "We have a tremendously caring and inspirational senior leader who is building an amazing community in our department. It is energizing to help him create an environment where our team is doing great work, is fully engaged, and feels like we can fulfill our professional goals."

What's important is that employees have the *perception* that their environment allows them to meet their ABC needs. Leaders and teams need to be mindful of the conditions that increase the likelihood that the ABC needs will be met. They are as follows:[15]

- Having meaningful goals that all team members work toward;
- Having manageable challenges with gradually increasing new challenges that progressively stretch and expand team member's skills;
- Having mentoring and support from leaders who express an autonomy supportive leadership style (see chapter 6 for specific strategies to build this leadership style);
- Having positive, high-quality connections with collaborators (social interactions are encouraged, a more challenging aspect amid COVID-19);
- Having access to training and development opportunities.

In addition, the following work factors also satisfy ABC needs and build thriving, the powerful combination of vitality plus learning and growth.[16]

Decision-Making Discretion

Decision-making discretion builds autonomy and competence. Professionals (especially junior team members) have freedom to make choices about how to do their work without pressure or micromanagement. (COVID-19 has proved that this can be done effectively.) They are free to seek out new work and build their skills. Leaders can help by defining the outcome of a project or specific parameters but letting team members create the process to get there.

Broad Information Sharing

Sharing information consistently within your team also builds autonomy and competence. When professionals have enough information to do their jobs well, it increases the likelihood that they will make sound, informed decisions. In addition, they can uncover problems quickly and coordinate action, which is particularly valuable for preserving team resilience. Broad information sharing also allows individuals to increase their understanding of how their work fits into the larger work system.

Regular Feedback on Progress

Professionals need in-time feedback so that they can make progress on challenging goals and make adjustments as needed. It promotes belonging and competence. Feedback generally should be FAST—frequent, accurate, specific, and timely.[17] Constructive feedback should be delivered as a learning-focused two-way conversation. (You can find a template for facilitating these types of conversations in chapter 5.) Feedback also resolves feelings of uncertainty, which can prevent toxic thinking styles such as catastrophizing and counterproductive thinking shortcuts.

Good work outcomes happen when your ABC needs are met. So why, then, do so many managers still use the carrot-and-stick approach to motivation? Because it works—in the short term. Many leaders are under significant pressure and just want employees to get the immediate job done. I am reminded of my friend Dan, a retired sergeant first class in the US Army. He recalled the moment when he realized his troops were following him out of fear, rather than respect, and it sunk him. The carrot-and-stick approach will get you results in the short term, but you'll pay a price for it later.

Burnout Basics: Things to Remember

- ABC stands for autonomy, belonging, and competence.
- Psychological safety and ABC needs are the foundation of resilient, thriving, and high-performing teams. Leaders have a significant role to play in developing both of these areas, but there are simple strategies all team members can practice.
- Being accessible and approachable, limiting side conversations and gossip, and giving everyone on the team an opportunity to contribute an idea or voice a concern are some ways to develop psychological safety.
- Having meaningful goals, receiving in-time feedback, sharing information, and access to training and development opportunities are examples of strategies that build ABC needs.

Chapter 5

Relationships
The Importance of Building Connection

Think back to the last time you took public transportation. What were most people doing? If it's anything like the planes, trains, buses, and subways I ride (or used to, pre-COVID-19), people probably generally kept to themselves, working or scrolling through social media on smartphones.

But what if you were forced to interact with strangers? Behavioral science researchers at the University of Chicago conducted a series of experiments to test this very question.[1]

Hundreds of bus and train commuters were assigned to one of three conditions: (1) interact with a stranger; (2) remain disconnected (sit in solitude); or (3) commute as they would normally. In addition, a separate group of study participants were asked to predict which pathway would lead to the most positive experience. Although most participants predicted a more positive experience in solitude, the actual results were the opposite. Participants reported a more positive (and no less productive) experience when they connected with strangers.

The need to belong is a fundamental human motivation,[2] and teams and organizations need to prioritize it, starting with onboarding. The ways in which organizations and teams convey belonging (or not) and connection create strong mindsets in new hires that can significantly shape how they subsequently view the work environment. Relationships make up the "R" of the PRIMED model.

One thing that COVID-19 has exposed is how important in-person connection is at work and to work teams. We are experiencing an ever-changing "new normal" amid a pandemic that many thought would last no more than a handful of weeks, and teams have felt the lack of connection. Many tell me how much they miss the "water cooler" moments at work—bumping into a colleague to say hi or to share a new idea. Those spontaneous moments of innovation and spark have plummeted or been eliminated entirely, because they are hard to replicate virtually. The pandemic has also exposed the increasing problem of loneliness.

Loneliness at work can contribute to burnout[3] and depression[4] and has been found to be highest in law, engineering, and science-related fields.[5] In addition, loneliness influences work performance (lonely employees become less invested in the organization) and team dynamics (they are perceived to be less effective in their team role and may send emotional signals that cause team members to repel, increasing the emotional spiral of loneliness).[6] Loneliness is not caused by being alone but from a perceived lack of connection with others.[7] Loneliness can be eased with small acts of kindness, showing a genuine interest in another person while expecting nothing in return, mindset shifts and reframes, participating in groups that matter to you, offering encouragement to others, and capitalizing on positive events.[8] Importantly, most of these strategies are free or cost little and can be implemented in remote-work environments.

Important Ways to Increase Connection

Prioritize Connection in the COVID-19 "New Normal"

Good relationships with work colleagues are a critical job resource, instrumental in helping prevent burnout.[9] When I ask people to list their job resources in my workshops, almost universally people say that if it weren't for supportive colleagues and coworkers, they would have left an organization years ago. A group of nurses I worked with used the term "Code Green" affectionately to refer to their tight bond.

When I asked what that meant, one nurse responded, "That's the phrase we use when we all need to go out for margaritas!"

COVID-19 has shifted the way work gets done, and teams will continue navigating a new way of working that will likely involve some combination of in-person and virtual work. One of the companies taking the lead on this model is the travel tech company trivago. When I talked to its CEO, Axel Hefer, he said the company had a very strong culture of in-person togetherness, so they were skeptical about whether remote work would be successful. What they discovered was what many companies now tell me: Remote work can be done and done well, and teams appreciate and want the flexibility it affords. However, some problems emerged. Hefer noticed strategic discussions fell flat because the same level of energy was hard to reproduce remotely. Team members couldn't get a "read" on how others felt over remote platforms. Also, it was difficult to onboard new talent and develop "learning on the job." New hires need to be able to ask questions on the fly, and those small moments of connection are hard to engineer remotely. To address both the successes

---

Staying Connected on Virtual Teams

There are also additional considerations to think about for virtual teams because the virtual aspects of teaming can negatively impact psychological safety and cohesion.[10] To ensure trust, belonging, and connection, virtual teams must do the following:[11]

- Regularly revisit progress toward stated goals and objectives
- Celebrate milestones and small wins
- Respond to requests in a timely and meaningful manner
- Increase feedback
- Highlight times when team members provide important assistance across locations
- Be transparent—give regular context updates and updates on major changes in each location
- Be open and talk about the challenges your team faces working at a distance
- Regularly discuss your team's common purpose

and challenges, trivago created a hybrid model of work, which they are piloting. Employees will continue to work remotely but are strongly encouraged to be in the office one week per month. It is during this week onsite that all in-person feedback, monthly planning meetings, strategy workshops, team dinners, and events are scheduled. According to Hefer, "Nobody knows the perfect balance, and it will be different for each organization and each team. And it might take a long time to find the right approach." Trivago is committed to trying new methods, getting feedback, and iterating when needed. Connection is that important to their culture.

Capitalize on Each Other's Good News

Sharing positive events and good news with work colleagues provides personal and relationship benefits. Sharing good news with another person increases the perceived value of the event, promotes trust, and increases the likelihood that you'll help others.[12] In a series of studies, participants were asked to recall one of their most positive moments from the past few years. Participants were paid a modest sum of money for participating in the experiment, and after completing the experiment and a related questionnaire, they were purposefully overpaid. Sixty-eight percent of the participants who received an enthusiastic reaction to their good news returned the overpayment, compared to 35.9% of the participants who received a disparaging reaction and 47.7% who received neutral feedback.[13]

Responses to good news must be both active and constructive (rather than passive and destructive) to build relationships, and each response style has certain characteristics (see table 5.1).[14] Included in the table is also an example of each response type to the good news that you are telling your team that you just got promoted.

I've been teaching this skill for years, and it's harder than it looks. To be effective, you have to know what your Active Constructive Responding (ACR) roadblocks are. Table 5.2 includes the common ones.[15]

Table 5.1. Response Styles to Good News

Active Constructive ("Joy Multiplier")[16]	Active Destructive ("Joy Thief")
• Responder asks questions and additional details • Asks about the underlying meaning of the event SOUNDS LIKE: "Congratulations. It's well-deserved. Tell us more about your new role. How are you going to celebrate?"	• Points out negative implications • Minimizes the event's significance SOUNDS LIKE: "That's impressive, but don't you already have too much on your plate? You were just telling us how exhausted you've been. Are you sure this is a good move?"
Passive Constructive ("Faux Listener")	**Passive Destructive ("Response Shifter")**
• Very little is said • The good news is acknowledged but there may be silence SOUNDS LIKE: "That's nice."	• The good news is ignored altogether • Responder directs the conversation to something else about him or her SOUNDS LIKE: "That reminds me, I have to go talk to HR about some questions I had regarding my last performance review."

Table 5.2. Reframing ACR Roadblocks

ACR roadblock	Reframe
I'm too busy.	You don't have to have an extended conversation with the sharer. Be curious and ask one more question than you otherwise would have.
I don't care about the good news.	This skill isn't about the news—it's about the person. The news is simply a conduit to facilitate connection.
I have concerns about the good news, or there is a disconnect between my values and the sharer's values.	Sometimes a person's good news might be legitimately concerning. The rule of thumb here is Conversation A and Conversation B—use ACR, then follow up separately about your concerns.
The good news isn't obvious, or I don't know what it means.	This isn't a "fake it till you make it" skill. Ask clarification questions.
The news isn't good enough to justify a response.	A lawyer told me this was why he didn't use ACR. Just don't be this person. Your job is not to rank or judge the quality of the other person's good news.
The good news makes me jealous.	Although you have to examine the root cause of your reaction, the sharer has some responsibility too. If you find out you're pregnant with baby number three, consider how you will share the news with your friend going through IVF.

Teaching this skill has taught me a lot about the power of missed moments. My dad is retired and often called me in the afternoon to talk about his day. My default response style was usually passive constructive ("faux listening"), to the point where I eventually noticed that he was calling me less. I called him and asked why he wasn't calling as frequently, and he said, "It just doesn't seem like you have enough time for me." Ouch. If you are unable to briefly acknowledge another person's good news, sharers will find other people—just like my dad did. Think about what that means as a leader, team member, parent, and friend.

This skill also inspired one of the US Army soldiers we taught to reach out to his sister. He explained that his mother's death had created a rift in the family; as a result, he hadn't spoken to his sister in years. On our course day off, he took the train from Philadelphia to New York City and showed up at his sister's apartment building, unannounced. She was home, opened the door, and burst into (happy) tears.

Debrief

Teams that regularly huddle or debrief about important goals, for key decision points, and at the end of projects have higher levels of trust and less burnout.[17] Why? The process of formally reviewing an event enhances team members' sense of control (I know what's expected of me and what I need to do) and support (my team members have my back).[18] An After-Action Review (AAR) is a common method of debriefing that originated in the military but is widely used in the business world today. Here are some questions your team can ask:[19]

1. What was the intended outcome?
2. What was the actual outcome?
3. What specific actions and behaviors helped/didn't help?
4. What went well?
5. What would we do differently?

Because workplace teams are busy, it's important to know that debriefs don't have to take a long time—most average about 15 minutes. In addition, although I've established this as a team skill, you can and should start to use AAR for your own performance on projects. After every speaking engagement, I make note of what went well and what I want to do differently in future trainings.

Talk to Each Other About Stress (and the "Hard Stuff" Generally)

One of the questions I'm most frequently asked to explain at workshops is how both leaders and team members can talk to each other about stress, particularly when it becomes more obvious that a leader or team member is struggling. Many of the teams I work with rank themselves low in their ability to have difficult conversations within the team. A team at a large financial services corporation I worked with called it a "culture of nice"—meaning they were so worried about being nice to each other that they avoided saying the things that needed to be said.

Though you may be worried about addressing stress-related concerns, many people I have interviewed (myself included) report that they wished a trusted colleague would have said something. I recently worked with a team at a large West Coast–based bank, and one of the senior vice presidents said how appreciative she was that her colleague pulled her aside to express concern about the way she was handling stress. (Those subtle eye rolls and smirks get noticed!) Her colleague said, "You remind me of my third-grade teacher, and that's not a good memory!" The following is a framework to help.[20]

Before the Conversation: You don't want to "wing it." The first question you have to answer is whether you're the right person (or who is the right person) to have the conversation. You should then choose the time and location with care and intentionality and think about your goals for the conversation. Is there a behavior you want to see stopped or started? Or, are you just trying to let the person know you care?

One thing that impedes the ability to communicate is the human tendency to think we're right. That means you may listen to fix (your purpose is to solve a problem) or listen to win (your purpose is to win or to convince the person of something). The way to change this default is to listen to learn (your purpose is to put solutions aside and really try to understand the other person's world). Listening to learn becomes critical when talking to other people about stress. Simple cues such as, "I'm curious about that" or "Help me understand" can activate listening to learn.

Having the Conversation: STEP 1: Communicate the issue using facts. Discuss what you observe about the situation using concrete terms and facts and avoiding exaggeration and subjective impressions.

STEP 2: Address your concerns objectively. Express how you feel without blame and use phrases such as "I see" or "I feel."

STEP 3: Specify concrete next steps or actions. Ask for the other person's perspective (using a listen to learn mindset). Remember, this a two-way conversation. Discuss any issues or behaviors that must be addressed and discuss consequences (if appropriate).

STEP 4: Evaluate outcomes and goals. Both people should summarize the discussion to ensure clarity about next steps.

One salesperson walked up to me after a conference about five years ago. "If something doesn't change in my work in the next six months, I'm going to have a heart attack," he said. When burnout gets bad enough, people can experience serious health- and work-related consequences. So push through the discomfort and have the conversation—the time you give another person is worth it.

Work relationships require effort, but they are a critical job resource that helps you and your team prevent burnout.

Burnout Basics: Things to Remember

- Creating connection and prioritizing relationships at work are key job resources that build resilience and prevent burnout.

- Experiment with hybrid approaches to work so that connection isn't engineered out of work in the new normal prompted by the COVID-19 pandemic. Also pay attention to how connection is fostered on virtual teams.
- You can increase connection by making sure to capitalize on positive news, prioritize team debriefs, and talk about stress (and the hard stuff generally) on your team.

Chapter 6

Impact
Why Do You Do What You Do?

I was sitting at a table full of drill sergeants having lunch in the basement of the Sheraton Hotel in Philadelphia on the University of Pennsylvania campus. Lunch started like it usually did. I asked the soldiers how the training was going, fielding their questions and comments. And we talked about football, one of my favorite topics.

Out of the corner of my eye, I noticed one of the soldiers staring at me, his gaze not once leaving my face. After a few minutes, I turned to him and asked, "Hey, sergeant, what's up?" His immediate response was, "Are you just in this for a paycheck?"

I had never been asked that, and it caught me off guard. I did have a deeper reason for being part of this work. I told the sergeant about my grandpa, explaining that he was a World War II veteran who fought on D-Day and at the Battle of the Bulge and earned a Purple Heart for his valor. He was severely wounded and spent months healing his physical injuries, but he struggled with emotional wounds that never healed. That had an impact on my family, I explained, and if I could help just one soldier have a better response, it would be a great honor and a testament to my grandpa's legacy.

"That's a great story," he said, and I could see a shift in his demeanor. Shortly thereafter, he started asking me more questions, and I could tell he started to trust me.

How would you answer the sergeant's question? Why do you do what you do? Do you talk about the impact your team makes and the meaning you get from your work?

The Importance of Meaning

Work is an important source of impact for people, which is the "I" of the PRIMED model. It also includes meaning.

Meaning is personal—it's the subjective experience you have that your work matters, facilitates personal growth, and is significant and worthwhile.[1] Research has consistently linked meaning at work to dedication to one's career, willingness to put extra effort into your work role, organizational commitment, and intrinsic work motivation.[2] People who report having meaningful work have lower rates of absenteeism and higher levels of both objective and subjective job performance.[3] One study showed firefighters with higher levels of meaning were significantly less likely to burn out compared to their colleagues with lower meaning scores.[4]

These strategies will help you explore ways to develop more meaning.

Develop a Leadership Style That Supports Meaning and Motivation

Meaning is closely linked with motivation, and motivation can either be high quality or low quality.[5] High-quality motivation (also called intrinsic motivation) happens when your work aligns with personal values, has personal significance, and is fun and interesting.[6] High-quality motivation is negatively related to emotional exhaustion and turnover and positively related to persistence and innovation.[7]

Leaders can increase the likelihood their teams will experience meaning and motivation by developing the behaviors that create a "Leading to Support" leadership style (rather than a "Leading to Control" style). You know you are in the presence of a supportive leader when you hear team members describing that person as encouraging, inspiring, and caring. People will move mountains for leaders like this. In addition to fostering more meaning and motivation, a Leading to Support style leads to employee well-being and

Table 6.1. Comparing Leadership Styles

"Leading to Support" behaviors	"Leading to Control" behaviors
Acknowledge and listen to workers' perspectives	Be prescriptive, inflexible, and rigid in tone, communication style, and interactions
Encourage self-initiation; provide choices and opportunities for initiative	Scrutinize employees' slightest actions
Respond to questions; offer assistance and guidance as needed. Take a coach approach to problem-solving, which can be as simple as being a sounding board for someone and then shifting the conversation toward a specific outcome[11]	Pressure individuals to think, feel, or behave in certain ways
Provide a rationale or explanation for projects, goals, and big-picture vision	Use corrective or other punitive action intended to restore the behavior back to its desired outcome when leader demands are not followed
Clarify confusion and missing information related to roles and tasks	Create a competitive, individual-oriented environment

work engagement, positive organizational commitment, and prosocial behavior.[8] Importantly, the traits and behaviors associated with the Leading to Support style can be developed and improved (this is a great topic for coaching).[9] Table 6.1 compares the different styles.[10]

Follow the 20% Rule and Make Microchanges

Take a moment and list the specific aspects of your work that you find most meaningful. A physician might list patient care, research, educating future doctors, and/or making scientific discoveries. Lawyers may list drafting persuasive documents, litigating in court, mentoring new lawyers, and/or interacting regularly with clients. Now estimate the percentage of time you spend in each of those areas.

Is there disconnect between what you listed as meaningful and how much time you spend in that area? For many people, the answer is yes. Professionals who spent less than 20% of their time on their most meaningful aspect of work had almost double the rate of burnout as colleagues who spent closer to 20% of their time focused on a meaningful area.[12]

Some people find that to get close to 20%, they have to make microchanges in the way they work. Here are some ideas:

- Block off chunks of time on your calendar. Writing is one of the most rewarding aspects of my own work, but it will never happen unless I protect space on my calendar for it.
- Reorder your day. Prioritize your most meaningful tasks right away so that you're sure they get done and are not left to the chance of the day.
- Talk as a team about the aspects of your work that you either enjoy or dislike. You may be able to swap different tasks or change how you collectively tackle different projects.[13]

The Importance of Impact

Though meaning is more personal, impact is about others. An emerging fourth need to the ABC needs framework is beneficence—the sense that you are having a positive impact on others.[14]

We often had special guests join army resilience training days, but one such training included two special participants—the 14th Sergeant Major of the Army, Raymond F. Chandler III, and his wife, Jeanne. The sergeant major of the army (SMA) is the highest-ranking enlisted soldier. As the SMA prepared to leave, he called all the training team to the front of the main room. We didn't know what was going on. After a few words, he gave each of us one of his coins—the US Army's symbol of recognition, gratitude, and hard work. He shook each of our hands and thanked us for our service to our country. That coin is one of my most treasured possessions, and the moment is one I will remember for the rest of my life. Research suggests that although we adapt to money pretty quickly, we never quite get used to knowing we've made an impact.[15]

Here are ideas to get your team started.

Get Inspired by Your "End User"

I got real-time feedback from the SMA about my impact, but many people work without ever knowing the impact they have on others. Nurses, for example, don't always directly see or feel the benefit of the good they do for their patients (though the pandemic has revealed many such moments). Nurses care deeply about patient well-being, but regulations and paperwork have changed the way and the amount of time they work with patients.

Harvard Business School professor Jon Jachimowicz led a study that exposed a feedback disconnect between nurses (who didn't think they were providing value or care to their patients) and their patients (who thought their care was excellent). To fix this, the hospital CEO sent a letter to each discharged patient, which included a list of the nurses who provided care along with a note saying that the nurses would welcome an update about how each patient was doing. To make it even easier, a self-addressed, stamped postcard was included with the letter. About 20% of the patients returned the postcards including glowing feedback about the care they received, which not only bridged the impact gap the nurses felt but also led to a noticeable reduction in burnout and turnover intention.[16]

Other studies have replicated this impact gap effect. When university call-center employees heard directly from a scholarship recipient who shared a five-minute story about how he had benefited from their endless hours of cold-calling alums, their average time on the phone increased 142%, and they had 171% higher weekly revenues.[17] When radiologists saw a patient's photo in their medical file, they wrote 29% longer reports and achieved 46% greater diagnostic accuracy in reviewing CT scans.[18]

These ideas will help you and your team operationalize impact:[19]

- Visit your end user from time to time (and especially during COVID-19, you should be checking in on your end users virtually and with frequency).

- Become a client or customer, if you can. Using your own organization's products and services can help you understand the consequences of your job.
- Invite end users to visit your organization (these visits can be virtual) and share a powerful story about your product or service; ask for testimonials.
- Encourage team members to share their own stories of making a difference.
- Include a photo in a file.
- Know your client's story and share it when you assign projects.
- Follow up with your clients after a project has ended.

Know the Mission

You met trivago CEO Axel Hefer in the last chapter. I also talked to him about the importance of meaning, purpose, and impact during the pandemic—specifically, whether those things are really important in a crisis, when so much focus should be on short-term, day-to-day operations and the health and well-being of employees. He said purpose and impact have helped his teams stay motivated during COVID-19. As a business tied directly to the travel industry, their work disappeared within weeks. Trivago's mission is to "Empower people to get more out of life," and for them, this moment of adversity only highlighted why it matters to travel. Not spending time with people you love is literally the opposite of what the organization sees as important about travel—collecting new experiences together. Rallying around this mission motivated their teams because it forced them to think about the future of travel and what will matter to their customer a year from now and beyond. His teams started to think more innovatively about what those future needs might be and how trivago could influence those future needs. That's where they now focus their time and energy, driven by the larger organizational mission, which grounds the teams and their new work direction.

The way in which your organization impacts the world becomes an important anchor in times of crisis and adversity. How do your employees, leaders, and teams live the mission? Do they even know what it is?

Create a Larger-than-Team Goal

Although this strategy has been written about with an individual focus, I've adapted it to help your team think about the positive impact it wants to have within the organization.[20] To help your team get started, here are a few questions to consider:

1. What is the positive impact your team wants to have in the organization and within the division or larger work unit?
2. What are your team's values, and how are they lived?
3. What type of positive change do you want to make or create within the organization, division, or larger work unit? (See chapter 9 for more ideas.)
4. What would your clients, customers, or patients say about how your team helps them?
5. How does your team support the greater mission of the organization?

Burnout Basics: Things to Remember

- Meaning is the subjective experience that your work matters, and impact is the sense that what you do helps others. These concepts are particularly important during times of adversity and crisis.
- Leaders can (and should) develop a Leading to Support style that promotes meaning, engagement, motivation, and organizational commitment.
- The 20% rule with microchanges, connecting to your end user, and having larger-than-team goals help to build meaning and impact.

Chapter 7

Mental Strength
Or, Your Mind on Milkshakes

Take a moment and think about a milkshake. Imagine the delightful combination of milk and ice cream topped off with whipped cream and hot fudge oozing over the side of the glass. Milkshakes aren't known for being light in calories, and for most people, they are a summertime treat. To illustrate the importance of mindset, psychologists used milkshakes to test whether satiety could be manipulated based on the mindset of the person consuming the shake.

They split participants into two groups, and both groups were given the same exact 380-calorie milkshake. However, one group was told the milkshake was a 620-calorie indulgent shake (mindset of indulgence) and the other was told they were drinking a more nutritious, 140-calorie sensible shake (mindset of sensibility). Each shake was labeled with either a graphic depicting a delicious shake (like the one I described above) and the words "Decadence You Deserve" with the 620-calorie nutritional profile—or a graphic with no picture showing the words "Sensi-Shake—Guilt Free Satisfaction," with the 140-calorie nutritional profile. During the first interval, participants were asked to view and rate the label, and in the second interval, they were asked to drink and rate the milkshake. The mindset of indulgence group produced a dramatically steeper decline in ghrelin, a hormone that signals fullness, such that the lower the level, the more energy sufficiency or satiety you experience. Meanwhile, the mindset of the sensibility group produced a relatively flat ghrelin response. Remember, the shakes in both groups were identical. Mindset was the only difference in determining whether participants felt full or not.[1]

Mental strength is the PRIMED model's "M." The way you and your team think about stress has an enormous effect on how stress is experienced, with downstream effects on judgment, your health, performance, and even aging.[2] How teams think and importantly, how team members think together, significantly impact a team's ability to perform well and stay resilient.[3]

The most important mental strength skill you and your team can develop is to build your self- and team-efficacy, respectively, or what I call a Confidence Mindset.

Develop a Confidence Mindset

The research term for having a mindset of confidence is called "efficacy," and it exists at the individual and group levels.[4]

Self-efficacy is the belief in your ability to cope with a broad range of stressful or challenging demands and to succeed. Self-efficacy is negatively correlated with the exhaustion and cynicism components of burnout and strongly positively correlated with increased personal accomplishment, which makes it more likely that you will perceive your job demands as positively challenging and motivational.[5] Individuals with high self-efficacy are more likely to persevere, set courses of action that are personal and meaningful, and commit to challenging goals and good risks.[6]

Efficacy doesn't just exist at the individual level though. It is just as beneficial for teams. Team-efficacy is the team's shared belief in its ability to perform a task and to perform it well. Highly confident teams are more likely to actively engage in their work and proactively interact with each other, exhibit staying power when team efforts fail to produce quick results or are met with opposition, and have higher team resilience.[7] In addition, professionals who are part of highly confident teams experienced lower levels of emotional exhaustion.[8] Don't discount team setbacks and failure—adversity also acts as an important source of team-efficacy.[9]

Efficacy is usually context specific. You might feel highly confident about giving presentations at work but less confident about losing weight. Similarly, your team might feel confident designing new software but not so much at having difficult conversations with each other. The good news about efficacy, though, is that it's sticky. As you learn new skills and master new challenges, your beliefs about your skills and capabilities generally increase, permanently changing what you believe you (and your team) are capable of.

What's helpful is that both self- and team-efficacy are built in the same way with these steps.[10]

Part 1: Select a Skill or Ability to Develop and Make a Goal

You first need to identify a skill or ability that you individually, or that your team collectively, needs to improve, and then set a specific goal for improvement. Table 7.1 provides examples of skills categories you may need to develop.

It's important to be as specific as possible with this step. If you want to improve your leadership development, for example, that's a very broad set of abilities. Which specific area of leadership development do you want to improve? Similarly, if your team wants to get better at communicating, what aspect of communicating must

Table 7.1. Skills Categories to Develop

Self-efficacy—category ideas	Team-efficacy—category ideas
Well-being	Communication
Leadership development	Getting to know everyone on the team better
Business development	Developing resources
Time management	Trust
Public speaking	Celebrating wins/offering thanks and gratitude
Relationship building	Motivation

improve? Effective listening? Giving feedback? Receiving feedback? Getting better at having tough conversations?

Part 2: Use One or More of the Following Pathways to Develop the Specific Skill You Selected

Once you have identified a skill or ability to improve and framed your goal, now you need to develop it. Each of the following pathways can help you and your team get there, but some are more effective than others. These pathways are presented in order of effectiveness, from strongest to weakest:[11]

Pathway 1: Learn by doing (most effective). Practicing the skill you want to develop is the best way to increase efficacy. Based on what you selected in Part 1, list specific ways you/your team can build this skill by actually doing something.

Let's say you want to develop your public speaking efficacy. You may decide to join a National Speaking Association chapter near you, complete a request for proposal to speak at an industry-specific conference, or volunteer to lead next month's team meeting.

Pathway 2: Learn by watching and observing others. Watching other people or teams do the thing you want to get better at is powerful.

- Who is the excellent example to serve as your model?
- What specific actions do you want to observe?
- How will you make that happen?

Using the public speaking example, you may decide to watch TED Talks of your favorite speakers to see how they incorporate humor or stories into their presentations or take notes about your favorite speaker's style at your next work conference. My coaching client Brad wanted to get better at delivering feedback to his team. When we walked through this framework, he quickly remembered a boss who he thought was superb at giving feedback. He decided he was going to "interview" his boss about this feedback style and incorporate some of the strategies he learned into his own goals.

Pathway 3: Learn by being coached by a credible and respected source about your efforts. Getting feedback about your efforts is the third way to build efficacy.

- Who is the person or people you want to give you feedback about your efforts?
- How will you seek out this help or coaching?

You could record yourself giving a five-minute talk about your favorite topic and show it to a trusted friend for some feedback. You may also decide to hire a professional coach to give you some pointers.

Not all the pathways apply to the area of efficacy you or your team wish to develop. One of my workshop participants decided to improve his sleep efficacy. He got through "learn by doing" pretty easily as he developed some specific goals about new sleep habits he wanted to try. Observing others and getting feedback about his sleep patterns were more challenging—how was he going to "get feedback" about his sleep? If you discover that about the area of efficacy you or your team wants to develop, go with the best pathway available.

There are other important skills associated with building mental strength, and it starts with self- and team awareness. From there, you can implement action-oriented thinking and limit catastrophizing. But first, you need to know what undercuts mental strength for you and your team.

Know the Factors That Undercut Your Mental Strength

These are common situations that can weaken mental strength.[12] Maintaining my mental strength becomes much more effortful if items 1 or 3 on the list below are present.

1. You are in an unclear situation.
2. You are stressed and/or low on energy.
3. You are doing something for the first time.
4. Something that you value is at stake.

Discuss this as a team. If you know that unclear directions lead to rush judgments and stress for most of your team, then you can be more intentional about making sure that instructions are transparent and clear.

Use Action-Oriented Thinking

One of the most helpful groups of mental strengths strategies known to prevent burnout are those rooted in cognitive behavioral science.[13] The US Army resilience training focused heavily on these skills.

This model is meant to be applied to the more complex challenges that you and your teams regularly face.[14] When you or your team are stuck dealing with a setback or challenge, go through each of these steps.

CONTROL: What aspects of this setback or challenge can you control or influence?

RESOURCES: What resources are available to you? What people can help? Have you experienced anything like this before? If yes, what did you do?

DOWNSIDE: What can you do to reduce the potential downside of this setback or challenge? What are the lessons you can learn and leverage?

UPSIDE: What potential good can come from this? What opportunities might it present for you or your team?

ACT: What action steps can you take in the short term? Long term? What kind of plan do you need to create? What first steps can you take today?

Even the most mentally strong of us can get caught up in worst-case scenario thinking. The last skill I want to share is how to limit this rigid style of thinking. It's one of the most popular skills I teach.

Limit Catastrophizing ("Worst-Case Scenario Thinking")

Worst-case scenario thinking[15] is what happens when you encounter a stressor or challenge, and in five minutes, your brain spins a story that ends with you living in a van down by the river. (Did you catch the *Saturday Night Live* reference?) When you catastrophize, your thoughts often take one of two forms—you might downward spiral (in which one worst-case scenario thought leads to another, then another, to form a more progressively negative story) or have scattered thoughts (your brain sends forth lots of random worst-case scenario thoughts that don't link in any particular way).

Importantly, the stress-producing event doesn't have to be a big one. When I was invited to participate in my first resilience training with the soldiers, I was nervous. I didn't know much about the military, and as a former lawyer I worried that the soldiers wouldn't respect me. In addition, drill sergeants scared me because all I knew about them was from what I saw in the movies, and they seemed a tad intense. The night before the training started, our team hosted a meet-and-greet for our new class. As 180 soldiers filed in the basement of the Sheraton Hotel on the University of Pennsylvania campus, I scanned the room hoping to find some soldiers who "looked nice." I zeroed in on two of them, walked up, and said, "Hi, I'm Paula. Welcome to the training. What do you do?" One soldier looked at me and barked, "Ma'am, I'm a 36 Delta, a Pathfinder, and this is my buddy here, he's a 68 Whiskey, Ma'am!" My mouth fell open for a moment, and I furiously tried to translate his words into civilian English. That moment sank me, and I instantly started to catastrophize.

Stress-producing events can take many forms, like calling someone important by the wrong name, or getting a terse email from your boss saying, "Come see me now." Other stress-producing events might be having too much—or even too little—work. And, of course, the COVID-19 pandemic has produced a slew of new stressors, such as trying to balance work and homeschooling kids.

The top portion of figure 7.1 shows the steps you can take to balance your thinking (working from left to right). The bottom portion

Figure 7.1

Write down all of your worst-case thoughts **(HORROR MOVIE)**

Make up an equally unlikely positive story to get a boost of positive emotion **(DISNEY MOVIE)**

List the most likely outcome using just the facts **(DOCUMENTARY)**

Worst-case thoughts: (horror movie)	Best-case thoughts: (Disney movie)	Most likely outcomes: (documentary)
I'm going to get fired before I even start.	The soldiers will give me the highest marks of any trainer in the course.	I'll continue the conversation later in the training week.
The soldiers won't respect me.	I'll be promoted to teach the entire program by the next training!	I need to get more fully prepared for these trainings.
I'll get fired after the training for bad reviews.		I'm going to be a little nervous—I need to plan for those emotions.
I'll have to go back to practicing law.		

of the figure includes what I mapped out after my drill sergeant meet-and-greet.

In the end, this is what my plan of action looked like:

- Review the course training materials I received and review the US Army acronyms.
- Talk to my other training team colleagues to get some advice and best practices.
- Use a little self-compassion—you're starting a new job and learning a new language!

Mental strength is an important, but often overlooked, aspect of team thriving and resilience. When you deal with such complex and high-stakes matters, you must be able to look at challenges from multiple perspectives to think creatively and flexibly. Mental strength is also a valuable source of energy, our topic for the next chapter.

Burnout Basics: Things to Remember

- Mental strength has a huge impact on how you and your team experience stress.
- Self- and team-efficacy represents a belief in your ability, whether individually or collectively, to cope with a broad range of stressors.
- Counterproductive thinking is triggered by certain factors, and when you experience it, you can use action-oriented thinking to help get unstuck.
- Worst-case scenario thinking prevents you and your teams from being able to take purposeful action and perform well. There is a simple process, though, to help you recognize and modify this thinking style.

Chapter 8

Energy
Addressing Sources of Stress

G ood leadership can make all the difference in whether your teams experience burnout, but never has it been more important than in healthcare during the COVID-19 pandemic. Dr. Michele "Micki" Fagan is an emergency room physician at Maimonides Medical Center in New York City, who in early 2020 found herself in the center of the crisis. When I asked her to think about factors driving burnout on teams, meaning at work, what makes for a good physician leader, and managing significant levels of stress, she emphasized a few key themes: nondefensive communicating, frequent debriefing, checking in on each other, admitting failures and trying to learn from them, and prioritizing self-care, many of which are themes in this book.[1]

What struck me, though, were the comments from her colleague, Dr. Christine Rizkalla, when asked the same question.[2] Instead of a pandemic-related example, she told me about an event in 2019. She is an attending physician and associate program director in pediatric emergency medicine at Maimonides Medical Center, and her team had been trying to process an infant death. She asked the newer doctors, "Have you ever seen this before?" They started to cry. She said there is a stereotype that to provide good care, doctors have to be somewhat emotionally distant and move on to the next patient. "That is unrealistic and something you never get used to," she said.

Being open and talking about stress, the fact that leaders have bad days, the difficulty of the job, and the humanity behind witnessing trauma and loss have helped make her a better leader. The authenticity draws other physicians to want to work with her. She said "showing that you're human" has never been more important than it is right now.

There are a number of different approaches to take when addressing sources of stress for teams. What I have discovered is that the burnout prevention conversation starts with good leadership and positive energy—the "E" in the PRIMED model.

Five Core Qualities for Leaders to Practice

Leadership is one of the strongest influences on how teams and team members adapt to stress. Bad leaders drain the life out of teams and cost organizations millions of dollars in the form of disengagement, absenteeism, turnover, and subsequent costs to recruit and train the replacement. Yet I find in my work that organizations are way too slow to address bad leadership problems, and the reasons are often similar: They've been "talked to," it's "just the way they are," or they "bring in a lot of money or clients." But the burnout problem will not be fully solved until organizations address this leadership gap.

Whether you realize it or not, burned-out leaders get noticed. In one study, leaders with higher burnout rates, lower professional fulfillments scores, and poorer self-care practices were assessed as more ineffective leaders by their team compared to leaders who had better managed their stress and felt professionally fulfilled.[3] Luckily, leaders can lead in a way that prevents burnout and boosts team effectiveness by focusing on these five qualities:[4]

1. Keep people informed (**Inform**)
2. Encourage team members to suggest ideas for improvement (**Engage**)
3. Have regular career development conversations (**Develop**)
4. Provide regular feedback and coaching (**Inspire**)
5. Recognize people for a job well done (**Recognize**)

Tame the Leader-Producer Dilemma

Although these five practices are simple, they can be hard for leaders to implement (or even focus on) because of the leader-producer dilemma. The dilemma occurs and worsens as people gain seniority and continue to need to "produce" client or technical work, as well as take on an increasingly long list of leadership, business development, and organizational responsibilities.[5] Moving from being individual contributors to team participants and leaders requires people to invest more time, focus, and thoughtful energy into the healthy functioning of teams. And when the stress of the "producer" part of the equation increases, the "leader" aspects can be neglected. Here are several strategies to help you tame this conflict:[6]

- Delegate and then check in "regularly," but cocreate a schedule with the people to whom you have delegated.
- Be clear about what resources you have and whether you need to add or find more (see chapter 9 for ideas).
- Create an agenda that sets out your most critical objectives, and then decide what actions to prioritize to meet these (a great spot for coaching).
- Have a network of support. Who will deliver tough messages to you if you get off track?
- Reserve time for reflection.
- Know your icebergs (or rules).

Two-Part Stress Awareness Test

Stress is important for leaders and teams to monitor because if a team leader or team member is burning out, or if the team itself is not functioning well, it's contagious. Other team members can "catch" the emotions and effects of the burnout or conflict. People who work in teams that have high levels of burnout have gone on to develop feelings of exhaustion and negative attitudes toward work.[7] People need quick ways to measure stress levels and whether they are thriving. There are two options.

OPTION 1: If you're wondering whether what you're feeling is just stress or if it's burnout, take a quiz. Researchers have been able to validate a nonproprietary, single-question item to help you quickly determine your stress level.[8] The question they validated is subjective, and it should be used only as a first point of entry toward understanding and assessing burnout.

Overall, based on your definition of burnout, how would you rate your level of burnout?

1 = I enjoy my work. I have no symptoms of burnout.

2 = Occasionally I am under stress, and I don't always have as much energy as I once did, but I don't feel burned out.

3 = I am definitely burning out and have one or more symptoms of burnout, such as physical and emotional exhaustion.

4 = The symptoms of burnout that I'm experiencing won't go away. I think about frustration at work a lot.

5 = I feel completely burned out and often wonder if I can go on. I am at the point where I may need to make some changes or may need to seek some sort of help.

OPTION 2: The other approach you can take is to determine whether you're thriving. You'll recall that thriving is the combination of vitality and learning and growth. To determine whether you are thriving on your team, at work generally, on a specific project, or in your relationships, ask yourself these three questions:

1. Am I energized by this?
2. Am I learning something?
3. Am I continuing to grow and develop?

Energy matters. Positive emotions are as contagious as negative emotions and can create positive outcomes, such as decreased conflict and improved cooperation.[9] However, human beings have a bias toward the negative—we are hardwired to notice, seek out, and remember negative events and information, and negative information is processed more thoroughly.[10] As a result, leaders and teams need to train their ability to notice, seek out, and remember positive events and information. Positive emotions act in a powerful way to help your team perform well, think creatively, stay resilient, and protect against burnout.[11] Collective positive emotions have been shown to be an important precursor to team resilience.[12]

Sweat the Small Stuff

When it comes to staying motivated and energized at work, you really do have to sweat the small stuff.[13] One of the single biggest things you and your team can do to create energy, motivation, and positive emotions is to make progress in your work.

Although it's nice to win a big trial, get a research grant approved, or experience a breakthrough, those big wins don't happen all the time. What does happen, though, are minor milestones and small wins along the way, and it's these small wins that often evoke outsized positive reactions. Another wonderful by-product of progress is self- and team-efficacy. Small wins help fuel the belief that you are on the right track and have the power to accomplish the goals you and your teams set. You can support your team's daily progress by making sure that the right types of ingredients support their work and the right type of interpersonal support exists. Factors that make progress more likely (all key themes in this and other chapters) include clear goals, having enough autonomy, sufficient resources, sufficient time to do the work, encouragement from leaders, recognition, and someone to talk to when you get stuck or encounter an challenging aspect of the project.

Know Your "Icebergs"

Icebergs are your core values and beliefs about the way the world should operate, and they can frustrate your ability to lead effectively, manage stress, and prioritize your well-being.[14] Icebergs exist at the individual, team, and organizational levels. Take a moment to visualize an iceberg—the small piece visible above the water line, but the biggest part that remains hidden under the water. Your core values and beliefs often operate outside of your conscious awareness (hidden under the water) as you go about your day, but they can be triggered in certain circumstances. Think back to a time when you overreacted (or underreacted) to something, noticed a pet peeve (for me, slow drivers in the left lane), or stewed about something days after it happened. These are all indicators of a lurking iceberg.

Here are some examples of icebergs:

- I always need to be in charge, or things will go wrong.
- I must have all the answers.
- If I can't do something perfectly, I shouldn't do it at all.
- If you want it done right, you've got to do it yourself.
- Failure is a sign of weakness.
- Strong people don't ask for help.

I call icebergs your "rules." These rules often include the words "always," "never," or "must." As a result, your rules can be too inflexible to allow you to perform the way you want and achieve good relationships. It's important for you to surface your rules, and once you do, you can evaluate them by asking these questions:

- Is this rule helping or harming? Is it getting me closer to, or further away from, the goals I want to achieve?
- Is this rule too strict or inflexible?
- How or when did the rule develop?
- How might I need to reshape my rule to make it more flexible?

Carrie is a senior leader coaching client of mine with 12 direct reports. When we talked, she identified one of her rules as: "You must always be responsive to clients." For her, this meant responding to client needs within hours—always. She realized this rule was causing her to favor team members who displayed similar behavior and to think negatively about her direct reports who had a slower response style. I encouraged her to pull the team together to collectively decide the appropriate time to respond to clients. That way, the entire team owned the decision, and it allowed her to reshape and relax how she applied the rule to her team.

If your team has high levels of psychological safety, I encourage you to talk about your rules with each other.

Recovering from Burnout

Dr. Fagan initially reached out to me because she wanted to know what to tell her doctors when they asked, "What can I do about burnout?" Recovering from burnout, much like preventing it, requires acknowledging all the factors that cause it. How you recover also depends on how burned out you are. Here are some ideas:

Individuals:
TIER ONE RECOVERY: Busy professionals have a cluster of traits that can impact burnout recovery. They have a hard time saying no, have a hard time asking for help, often have very narrow definitions of success, and over-rely on achievement to feel worthy.[15] Part of what has helped me not burn out again is that I now understand my "wiring." I recognize how my icebergs/rules interfere with my ability to take breaks. I am better aware of the triggers and stress-producing events that cause me to catastrophize and waste mental energy. I have increased my self-efficacy by improving specific skills I need to better manage my stress—such as having difficult conversations instead of stewing about hurts and wasting energy. I am clear about my values and find it easier to say no to things that don't align with them. I am better at asking for help, though it will never feel completely comfortable to me, and I have relaxed my perfectionistic standards. This is the deep work you must do to really recover and stay recovered from burnout. Yes, you need to delegate

more, prioritize self-care, and establish boundaries, but those things may not stick unless you have developed this foundation of self-awareness.

TIER TWO RECOVERY: Recovering from a serious case of burnout, as mine was, may also require more help and deeper conversations. As my burnout worsened, I regret not reaching out to a mental health professional to treat the anxiety I was experiencing. If you are experiencing anxiety, depression, or other mental health/substance abuse issues, please reach out for professional help. In addition, you may also need to strongly examine whether you are working on the right team, in the right department, at the right organization, or even in the right industry.

Leaders:
Leaders strongly influence whether burnout happens on teams and within organizations. As such, you must educate yourself about what burnout is and pay attention to how it appears in your teams. It's up to you to lead the way by creating more psychological safety on your teams, identifying the icebergs/rules that interfere with your ability to lead effectively, using a Leading to Support leadership style, prioritizing the ABC needs, and recognizing team members for good work. If you do nothing other than commit to improving the five leadership qualities I mentioned earlier, that alone will help. I taught a workshop recently where the VP said to the team, "I know our team has zero capacity right now, and our workload is increasing. I'm going to devote time in the next few weeks to plan for ways to find excess capacity for you as we head into next year." I wanted to reach through my computer and hug him because I have never heard a leader express this before, and it's so needed!

The sources of stress for individuals and leaders are many. Individuals burn out in part because of their "wiring," but the work environment plays a big role. So, my answer to Dr. Fagan is this: Much like what you would say to your patients, treating the symptoms is a start, but to truly fix the problem we have to also treat the underlying causes. Individuals, leaders, and teams each play an important role.

Burnout Basics: Things to Remember

- Leaders can improve their ability to influence team stress by focusing on five areas.
- As professionals assume more responsibility, they need to be aware of, and tame, the manager-producer dilemma.
- To prevent burnout, you have to build stress awareness by measuring your stress levels and determine if you're thriving.
- Small wins and breakthroughs create sustained motivation and energy for your team and must be talked about with regularity.
- Your icebergs (or rules) can positively or negatively influence how you lead and how you manage stress.
- Helping people recover from burnout also requires a systems-based, holistic response.

Chapter 9

Design
How to Create Positive Change

Your team's processes, rules, and general workflow influence whether team members thrive or burn out. Laura is a lawyer at a large insurance company, and I met her when I interviewed her prior to a speaking engagement. I was hoping to learn more about burnout, but she was so overjoyed by her work that I changed my questions. I wanted to know more about the ingredients that helped her feel so supported and joyful each day. Laura was a stay-at-home parent for nine years before going to law school, and she found a corporate legal position right out of law school. (This is uncommon in the world of law, where "in-house" roles are usually reserved for attorneys with at least several years of practice experience.)

"I have extreme variety in my work," she told me. "In-house work tends to have more variety overall, I think, but I've also been asked to change support areas several times in my nine years at this job. I like to think it is because I am agile and able to quickly become an expert in a new area, and because I can easily establish relationships with different types of people/clients. This means that I really don't have a chance to get bored. And if I start to feel that I need a challenge, I'll ask to try something new or to be involved in a new initiative. Another thing that contributes to my satisfaction is recognition and encouragement from my leadership."

What if you could design your team's culture so that everyone feels like Laura at work? The simple answer is this: you can. Design—the "D," and final letter, of the PRIMED model—is a powerful aspect of work that can enhance or erode your team's resilience and motivation and set up your employees for burnout.[1] Work design involves examining the way job tasks and roles are structured and the ways in which job characteristics impact how an employee experiences work. Work design may promote team and individual well-being or erode it.[2] Importantly, these are strengths-oriented processes that involve all team members, which means each person owns the outcome, making the tweak or change more likely to stick. In addition, don't focus on changing an entire aspect of your team's work all at once. Focus on TNTs—tiny noticeable things.

There are three ways that teams can redesign their work to support positive change. The first is a simple tweak teams can make—identifying and relying on their resources. Where applicable, I'll also show you how to apply these tools at the individual level.

Identify and Rely on Your Resources

For Your Team

Focusing on creating more job resources, rather than on decreasing job demands, increases the odds of preventing burnout.[3] High-performing teams have access to sufficient job resources, and they know about and take advantage of all the resources available. When teams have enough resources, it signals their work is important and valuable. When I say the word "resources" to you, what comes to mind? When I ask teams this question, people usually point to the tangible resources that they need to do their jobs well—finances, personnel, technology, or equipment. But resilient teams maintain both tangible and intangible resources, such as leader and peer support, emotional resources, and coming to a consensus about things such as goals.[4]

In addition to the job resources listed in chapter 1, this checklist will help you work together to identify other resources that your team can rely on to stay resilient and prevent burnout.

- Find aspects of your work that are consistently repetitive. Can any of these processes/instructions/flow charts be made into templates for easy access and sharing?
- Learn lessons from other challenges—which we've come to know as stories. Personal and collective stories help to access emotional resources, especially positive emotions. Where and how are these stories codified?[5] In my work with TD Bank, five members of the legal and operations team each recorded a three-minute video of themselves explaining how they successfully overcame a work-related challenge. We discovered that there was always a positive aspect of the challenge to leverage. One of the lawyers thought of herself like a quarterback on a football team. As a leader, she said, "It is my role to elevate the quality of the team by demonstrating an uncomplaining attitude myself, in an effort to foster positivity. I have learned that being authentic about challenges we all face . . . demonstrates a certain humility that fosters [resilience]."
- Know each other's strengths and your team's values. How are these values lived, and how are violations handled? How do you impart these values to new team members?
- Identify people internal to the organization that your team relies on to do its work well. I have talked to teams, for example, that don't know that the group has a marketing professional to help them with messaging.
- Determine the external partnerships you have created (or might need) to help your team work efficiently.
- Promote a culture of learning on your team. What training and development opportunities exist for team members, and are they aware of them?
- Put someone in charge of monitoring your industry for early signs of emerging issues.
- Determine how you will support each other when the going gets tough.

For You

If you're going through any type of challenge, change, or setback at work or in your personal life, making a list of your personal resources boosts resilience and helps prevent burnout.[6] This is an exercise I use frequently in my workshops and with my coaching clients. Think about these questions:[7]

- Who are the people you can reach out to for support?
- What are your strengths and how can you leverage them?[8]
- What are your financial resources?
- What are your sources of hope?
- Have you gone through something like this before? If yes, what lessons can you apply to this challenge? Do you know someone else who has been through the same setback who can help?
- How can this challenge open new doors?

Appreciative Inquiry

The second way to activate positive change is with a process called Appreciative Inquiry (AI). The AI framework is centered on four steps, called the 4-D model: Discovery, Dream, Design, and Destiny. (I've modified the last D to "Deliver.")[9] AI's assumption is simple: "Every [team] has something that works well, and those strengths can be the starting point for creating positive change."[10]

The following case study presents a team I facilitated through the AI 4-D process. AI summits can be various lengths (even multiple days), but I wanted to pare down the process to allow for a conversation that could happen among team members in an hour or two. This team works within one of the world's largest finance companies and has an important function within the organization. It wanted to be seen as more influential within the organization.

Discover: What Matters Most to Your Team?

It's always important to start by asking what matters most. People in different roles and functionalities have different thoughts about what's important, and you need to hear all of those in this step. This team shared what matters most: trust (defined as shared core values and the willingness to protect each other's commitment to those values); confidence in each other and with the team as a whole; having fun; developing a good team reputation and credibility within the organization; collaboration; delivering on the mission; valuing diversity and different viewpoints; and being open to sharing as what mattered most to them.

Teams must be able to cite specific examples or else what matters most simply becomes a collection of words. This team talked about specific times when they actively supported each other and offered diverse viewpoints, along with a project that worked well because they intentionally leveraged existing global resources.

Dream: What Do You Want Your Team to Look Like or Grow Into?

Now that your team has a sense of what matters, supported with specific examples, they are ready to talk about a future version of the team they could grow into. It was important for this team to become the most trusted group in their organization—a more finely tuned version with clarity around projects, vision, and alignment. To do that, they wanted to prioritize professional growth, education, leadership development, and skill building. In addition, the team was beginning to grow, and they didn't want to lose their core values in the change and increasing workload. To make this happen, they recognized the need for more diversity, more clarity and structure, and expectations and boundaries with each other and other teams.

Design: What Pathways Will Take You from Where You Are Now to the Future Team You're Hoping to Create?

Teams need to identify how they will get from Point A (where they are now) to Point B (the future team you want to create). This team realized that to be seen as influencers, they needed to make their team mission clearer and be much more explicit in talking about their team's expertise and why they add value. This had been unclear, and it negatively impacted other people's perception of the team. They realized they needed to enlist senior-level allies to help with this messaging. With that came the realization that they needed to modify educational materials and training to explain these priorities and goals to new team members.

It would be impractical to ignore the realities and obstacles that exist for teams as they go through this process. This team played a strategic role within the organization, and they managed and dealt with high-level and sensitive information. They realized that given the nature of their work, it was likely that other teams within the organization may see them as an obstacle. Unpredictable workflow also made their jobs difficult. And they realized that because they also do a lot of individual work and are geographically diverse, they feel disconnected from each other's expertise.

Deliver: What Changes Are You Actually Willing to Make (Focusing on TNTs)?

Here is where teams need to focus on TNTs to generate progress toward the goals and ideas that have been generated in the steps mentioned previously. This team decided to create a team website/portal/landing page, which included individual team member backgrounds, a myth-busting page, FAQs, examples of success, its mission, and "partner with" pages to learn more about them. Sharing personal stories on the new team website and informally meeting with colleagues would help others see them as more vulnerable and real, which they felt would increase the benefit of the doubt others would give to the team. They also took a step back to think about the messages the team might be sending to other teams that they either don't intend or are unclear. Creating templates would help them collect repetitive information and make it more likely they could respond to requests more quickly.

As you can see, the team got to some concrete action steps. Each team member took responsibility for enacting some aspect of the outcomes, which they continue to build out and build upon.

AI for You

You can use the AI framework as well to make a positive change in your own life or career by asking yourself these questions:[11]

- When you feel energized and engaged, what is happening?
- How do you need or want to grow in your work and life roles?
- How can you move from where you are right now to where you want to be?
- What obstacles might you encounter, and how will you manage them?
- What is one step you can take today to move closer to that future possibility?

Think (and Act) Like a Kindergartner

The last way you can support positive change on your team is to cultivate the mindsets that support it. You may have heard the phrase "design thinking" associated with conversations about innovation. Design thinking is simply a problem-solving process meant to help you generate options, test strategies, and get feedback in service of making a positive change. There are now a variety of books, courses, podcasts, and ways to find out more about this methodology. Instead, what I want to do is introduce you to the mindsets you need to practice to redesign effectively.[12]

One of my favorite ways to illustrate the power of these mind-sets is to tell you about the spaghetti tower marshmallow challenge.[13] The instructions are simple: Teams of about four people get 20 sticks of dried spaghetti, one large marshmallow, one yard of string, and one yard of tape. They have 18 minutes to build the tallest freestanding tower possible, and the only rule is that the marshmallow has to end up on top. This experiment has been run so many times, in so many settings, that there are a lot of data about team outcomes. I have taught this exercise to many teams of lawyers, and the results are telling. Most don't finish—they don't even produce a tower that can stand on its own. Of the teams that do finish, almost all fall well short of the tower height average listed. Here are some groups that succeed (and fall short):

- Teams of business school students: average towers less than 10 inches tall
- Teams of lawyers: average towers 15 inches tall
- Participants generally: average towers 20 inches tall
- Teams of CEOs: average towers 22 inches tall

But there is one group that tends to consistently outperform almost every group—teams of kindergartners! They average towers that are 26 inches tall. Why? They naturally act like designers and use these mindsets that are critical to making positive change:

- **MINDSET 1: Humble curiosity.**[14] Curiosity invites exploration. I work with a lot of advice-givers and experts who get paid lots of money to tell other people what they know. That is helpful in executing work but impedes positive change and redesign. Creating any type of lasting change on your team, whether big or small, starts by admitting you alone don't have all the answers and instead need to ask some questions. Talk to your patients, your business clients, your colleagues, and to each other and invite a deeper conversation. Sentence starters such as, "I'm wondering" or "Tell me more about that" signal that you're interested in learning more. Curiosity can be a superpower—curious people tend to enjoy complex thinking, tolerate uncertainty better, and have a tendency to avoid judging, criticizing, or blaming others.[15]

- **MINDSET 2: Try stuff**. Remember, teams have 18 minutes to complete the challenge. Most teams waste too much time discussing strategy and figuring out who's in charge. Start small with TNTs, such as asking questions and having conversations. For example, are people on your team asking for more flexibility about how and where they can work? Experiment with what that could look like. It's been most frustrating to see that it took a pandemic for teams and organizations to figure out what organizational research has been very clear about for years—that giving people flexibility about how and where to work are huge engagement and motivation boosters.[16]

- **MINDSET 3: Prepare to pivot**. Your small experiments will often fail or will at least have to be tweaked, but those lessons provide you with valuable data. Teams often get married to their first idea, but amazing ideas and new ways of doing things can come from the mess. When the kindergartners made mistakes with their spaghetti towers, they didn't get bruised egos or defensive; they just tried something different. Resilient teams pivot quickly: They don't have to go through three committees and twelve meetings to decide something. They act (in an informed way) and pivot.

- **MINDSET 4: Collaborate and ask for help**. You don't have to make a positive change by yourself, and often the best ideas are going to come from other sources. Creating positive change is a collaborative process, and you should rely on all the resources your team has at its disposal. I have also found that coaching (both with leaders individually and with the team in small groups) can be a tremendous asset for teams who want design efforts to stick.

If people are burning out on your team, something about your processes, rules, or the way you do things is off or must be tweaked. Changing the organizational culture as a whole will be difficult, but leaders have much more leverage if they focus on making TNTs at the team level.

Burnout Basics: Things to Remember

- You can actively create the type of positive culture that leads to less burnout and more well-being and thriving by using a few simple strategies.
- Resilient teams are well aware of all the tangible and intangible resources at their disposal.
- Appreciative inquiry questions help both you and your teams leverage strengths and what's going right on the team to design a stronger culture.
- Understanding the mindsets involved with creating a more positive team culture will help make the process more fun and likely to stick.

Conclusion

Preventing burnout requires that organizations shift from taking an individual-only approach to systems-based, holistic tools and frameworks that teams can employ to develop resilience and thriving. To help, I have given you almost two dozen research-based strategies to use, with some ideas about where to start. Your goal is to start with a few specific skills and build from there based on what your teams' needs and goals are.

When I work with organizations, I like to follow this process: (1) Assess burnout rates and causes in the team and have the team take my Resilient Teams Inventory; (2) educate team leaders and teams (either collectively or in separate trainings) about the burnout and resilience basics and unpack some of the strategies to give the team a common language to begin using; and (3) use postworkshop coaching to help those leaders and team members who are interested in either developing more skills or talking to me about a specific stressor or challenge. The coaching piece is an important part of the process, and one that I have found to be transformative.

Table C.1 lists the skills I recommend each group begin to develop.

I was on the verge of a breakdown when I stopped my law practice. I had gotten so far away from myself that I wasn't sure that I would find my way back. I was sick, cynical, and disconnected from the very people who wanted to help and support me. It shouldn't have to come to that. Continued flexibility, respect, transparency, feedback,

Table C.1. Next Steps: Start Here

Individuals	Teams	Leaders
Increase your self-efficacy (chapter 7).	Make debriefing a habit; talk as a team about how to implement (chapter 5).	Review the behaviors associated with psychological safety and tweak as necessary (chapter 4).
Identify the triggers that weaken your mental strength; limit worst-case scenario thinking (chapter 7).	Talk as a team about a skill/ability you need to develop and practice the team-efficacy exercise (chapter 7).	Give team members the autonomy quiz (chapter 4).
Detect your icebergs/rules (chapter 8).	Create a larger-than-team goal (chapter 6).	Review the five core qualities for leaders to determine what you need to improve (chapter 8).
Improve ACR and identify your ACR patterns (chapter 5).	Do you need to make any tweaks to your team culture? Start talking about the AI questions (chapter 9).	Review the Leading to Support behaviors and adjust as needed (chapter 6).

professional development opportunities, and recognition are simple behaviors every leader and organization can prioritize right now, all of which will inspire loyalty, motivate employees, and help to ease some of the stress people are feeling.

Burnout is a big problem, but there is something we can do about it. Let's start now.

Acknowledgments

We can only be said to be alive in those moments when our hearts are conscious of our treasures.
—Thornton Wilder

Writing a book is hard and stressful, and fun, and stressful! I am deeply grateful to everyone who made this book possible.

I know what it feels like to burn out, and it wasn't easy to tell my story many years ago. I'm incredibly thankful to all the people (strangers and clients alike) who have shared their stories with me so that I could help educate others about what burnout feels like. This book would not have been the same without your wisdom.

I have the best clients. I get to work with outstanding organizations, leaders, lawyers, healthcare providers, and professionals who dedicate themselves day in and day out to making other people's lives better. It has been such an honor to help you advance your causes, and I have learned so much from all of you.

I'm grateful to my editors at *Forbes*, *Fast Company*, and *Psychology Today* for giving me a platform to find my voice, raise awareness, and talk openly about burnout, work, stress, and resilience.

I have a fantastic team! Thank you Suzanne Kosmerl, Nancy Sheed, Tasha Bernard, Raquel Wilson, Alex Lerch, Kimberly Berger, and Sarah Koenig for keeping my head above water and helping me continue to grow my business. And a special shout out to my cousin Bettina Vanderloop for helping me organize hundreds of studies and random pieces of paper so that I could start writing. I would still be sifting through paper if you hadn't helped me!

This book would not have happened without Brett LoGiurato at Wharton School Press (WSP). He emailed me last year to say he had been following my work, and that WSP was considering publishing a book about burnout. He asked me to submit a proposal, and on November 6, 2019, I found out my proposal was accepted. I had just finished speaking at a conference and was listening to the next session when I read the email. I had to stifle my ugly cry as I realized in that moment that my dream of becoming a business book writer was going to come true. Thank you, Brett! Thank you also to the rest of the team at WSP, especially Shannon Berning. Your guidance has made this process so easy. I can't say enough great things about the folks at WSP—I truly value our partnership. And of course, thank you to my agent, Ivor Whitson, who took a chance on me many years ago and always believed there was a place in the literary world for a book about my take on burnout.

Mr. Rogers once asked an audience to pause and think about who loved them into being. I was only able to write this book because so many people have loved me into being.

I dedicated this book to my Grandpa Davis and his best friend, Ray. My grandpa never talked about his experiences in World War II, and I only recently learned a key piece of his story. My grandpa was not drafted into the war—he voluntarily enlisted. Why? So that his best friend, Ray, who was drafted, didn't have to go alone. If that's not the essence of friendship and love, I don't know what is. I couldn't be prouder to be your granddaughter.

My experience working with the men and women of the US Army, the DA civilians who support them, and the soldiers' spouses and family members is an experience I will treasure for the rest of my life. I learned from them the meaning of sacrifice, honor, loyalty, and what it means to be part of something bigger than oneself. Many of them have become close friends and are like family members. A simple thank you will never be enough to pay you back for putting your lives on the line so that I can enjoy the freedoms and privileges of this great country, but to all the soldiers I have worked with, thank you. Although I know I have missed many, I want the world to know your names: Dan Mason, Nate Kinnard, Brent Sicely, David Parish, Justin Daniels, Lauren Osinski, Christopher Poe, Randy Traxler,

Jennifer Ballou, Niki McFarland, Bill Loggins, Tim Frock, Michael Davis, Donna Brazil, Jay Nolet, Johnny Strickland, Teresa King, John Guna, Michael Flores, Richard Gonzalez, Stan Johnson, Nic Kletzien, Trevor Proefrock, Derek Eurales Jr., Sean Heath, Thomas E. Tucker Jr., Micheal Bird, Alexander Torres, Travis Enstrom, Ottis West, Roy Cantu, Michael Ballard, Don Grundy, Jordan Larson, Scott Gilbert, Scott Hellinger, and Keith Allen.

I would not have made it through each phase of my life/career journey without the love and support of my friends. They have held my hand, listened, wiped my tears, danced with me, celebrated life, encouraged, inspired, and pushed me when needed. Thank you, Julie Miller, Sylvia Lopez (also a soldier), Julie Haut, Wendy Althen, Kim Van Voorhees Bell, Tracy Sterken Perkins, Sharon Laatsch, Katrina Gustum Chovan, and John Ferko.

To my family, whose love and support grow more each year. Thank you to my mom, Trish Davis, my dad, Bob Davis, and my brother, Jeff Davis—you have always believed in me, always. And to my extended family of aunts, uncles, and cousins—thank you for all the family reunion fun and for being there for me when I needed it most. Extra big hugs to my precious nephew, Owen, and to my sister-in-law, Cortney Davis.

Tom—you get an extra big thank you. From day one, you have believed in my business and in this book. Writing this book became my second job, and that meant writing mainly on the weekends. You always asked me what I needed so that I had the time and space to write, knowing that Lucy was in good hands. I literally couldn't have done this without you.

And finally, to my dear daughter, Lucy Tess. I didn't think motherhood was going to be part of my journey for many reasons, but thankfully the universe had other plans. Out of the billions of people on the planet, we somehow found each other. I am so thankful to be your mom, and as I tell you every night before bed: Out of all the babies in the whole world, I got the best one.

Notes

Introduction

1 *Taking Action Against Clinician Burnout: A Systems Approach to Professional Well-Being* (2019). A Consensus Study Report, National Academy of Medicine. Retrieved on April 9, 2020, at http://www.nationalacademies.org/hmd/Reports /2019/taking-action-against-clinician-burnout.aspx.

2 Marcus Buckingham & Ashley Goodall (May 14, 2019). The Power of Hidden Teams. *Harvard Business Review.* https://hbr.org/cover-story/2019/05/the-power -of-hidden-teams.

3 *Id.*

4 Christine Porath, Gretchen Spreitzer, Cristina Gibson, & Flannery G. Garnett (2012). *Thriving at Work: Toward Its Measurement, Construct Validation, and Theoretical Refinement.* 33 Journal of Organizational Behavior 250–275. *See also* Anne-Kathrin Klein, Cort W. Rudolph, & Hannes Zacher (2019). *Thriving at Work: A Meta-Analysis.* 40 Journal of Organizational Behavior 973–999.

5 Stefan Razinskas & Martin Hoegl (2020). *A Multilevel Review of Stressor Research in Teams.* 41 Journal of Organizational Behavior 185–209.

Chapter 1

1 Names and identifying details for some people and teams have been changed. In certain instances, the stories are composites of one or two people I have interviewed.

2 Tait Shanafelt, Joel Goh, & Christine Sinsky (September 25, 2017). *The Business Case for Investing in Physician Well-Being.* JAMA Internal Medicine, Special Communication, E1–E7.

3 Harvard Medical School study reported on by Leslie Kowh (May 7, 2013). When the CEO Burns Out. *Wall Street Journal.* https://www.wsj.com/articles/SB100014 24127887323368760457846912400852469.

4 Laurence Bradford (June 19, 2018). Why We Need to Talk about Burnout in the Tech Industry. *Forbes.com.* Retrieved on April 20, 2019, at https://www.forbes .com/sites/laurencebradford/2018/06/19/why-we-need-to-talk-about-burnout-in -the-tech-industry/#7bd984901406.

5 American Federation of Teachers survey published in 2015.

6   Career Satisfaction and Retention—White Paper (June 2014). eFinancial Careers Survey. https://finance.efinancialcareers.com/rs/dice/images/eFC-US-Retention -2014.pdf.

7   Personal correspondence with Maj. Lauren A. Shure, Deputy Chief, Special Victims' Counsel Division, United States Air Force, from October 2019 through early 2020.

8   Andrew P. Levin et al. (2011). *Secondary Traumatic Stress in Attorneys and Their Administrative Support Staff Working with Trauma-Exposed Clients.* 199(12) Journal of Nervous and Mental Disease 946–955.

9   Anna Goldfarb (March 26, 2019). Stop Letting Modern Distractions Steal Your Attention. *New York Times.* https://www.nytimes.com/2019/03/26/smarter -living/stop-letting-modern-distractions-steal-your-attention.html. *See also* Anna Goldfarb (April 8, 2019). Turn Off, Tune Out, Unlink. Then Get Some Work Done. *New York Times,* Smarter Living section, page B6.

10 *Taking Action Against Clinician Burnout: A Systems Approach to Professional Well-Being* (2019). A Consensus Study Report, National Academy of Medicine. Retrieved on April 9, 2020, at http://www.nationalacademies.org/hmd/Reports /2019/taking-action-against-clinician-burnout.aspx.

11 Tait D. Shanafelt et al. (2010). *Burnout and Medical Errors Among American Surgeons.* 251(6) Annals of Surgery 995–1000.

12 Firm Administrator Conference of a large legal malpractice insurance carrier. August 2017.

13 World Health Organization (May 28, 2019). Burn-out an "Occupational Phenomenon": International Classification of Diseases. Retrieved on February 1, 2020, at https://www.who.int/mental_health/evidence/burn-out/en/.

14 Christina Maslach & Michael Leiter (2005). Stress and Burnout: The Critical Research in *Handbook of Stress, Medicine, and Health,* 2nd ed. (Cary L. Cooper, ed.) 155–170. Boca Raton, FL: CRC Press.

15 Wilmar B. Schaufeli, Michael P. Leiter, Christina Maslach, & Susan E. Jackson (1996). MBI-General Survey. You can purchase a license to use the MBI at www .mindgarden.com. Other psychometrically supported inventories that are publicly available include the Oldenburg Burnout Inventory and the Copenhagen Burnout Inventory.

16 Arnold B. Bakker & Evangelia Demerouti (2017). *Job Demands-Resources Theory: Taking Stock and Looking Forward.* 22(3) Journal of Occupational Health Psychology 273–285.

17 Arnold B. Bakker & Evangelia Demerouti (2007). *The Job Demands-Resources Model: State of the Art.* 22(3) Journal of Managerial Psychology 309–328.

18 Arnold B. Bakker, Evangelia Demerouti, & Ana Isabel Sanz-Vergel (2014). *Burnout and Work Engagement: The JD-R Approach.* 1 Annual Review in Organizational Psychology and Organizational Behavior 389–411. As to the

Core Six, *see also* Michael P. Leiter & Christina Maslach (2003). Areas of Worklife: A Structured Approach to Organizational Predictors of Job Burnout in *Emotional and Physiological Processes and Positive Intervention Strategies Research in Occupational Stress and Well-Being.* Volume 3, 91–134. *See also Taking Action Against Clinician Burnout: A Systems Approach to Professional Well-Being* (2019). A Consensus Study Report, National Academy of Medicine. Retrieved on April 9, 2020, at http://www.nationalacademies.org/hmd/Reports /2019/taking-action-against-clinician-burnout.aspx.

19 Tino Lesener, Burkhard Gusy, Anna Jochmann, & Christine Wolter (2020). *The Drivers of Work Engagement: A Meta-Analytic Review of Longitudinal Evidence.* 34(3) Work & Stress 259–278.

20 *Id.* at 275. *See also* Marc Van Veldhoven et al. (2020). *Challenging the Universality of Job Resources: Why, When and For Whom Are They Beneficial.* 69(1) Applied Psychology: An International Review 5–29.

21 Joel Goh, Jeffrey Pfeffer, & Stefanos A. Zenios (2016). *The Relationship Between Workplace Stressors and Mortality and Health Costs in the United States.* 62 Management Science 608–628.

22 Jeffrey Pfeffer (2018). *Dying for a Paycheck: How Modern Management Harms Employee Health and Company Performance—and What We Can Do About It* 46–47. New York: HarperCollins.

23 Michael P. Leiter & Christina Maslach (2000, 2011). Areas of Worklife Survey. You can purchase a license to use the AWS on www.mindgarden.com.

24 Julia Moeller et al. (2018). *Highly-Engaged but Burned Out: Intra-Individual Profiles in the US Workforce.* 23(1) Career Development International 86–105.

25 Denise Albieri Jodas Salvagioni et al. (2017). *Physical, Psychological and Occupational Consequences of Job Burnout: A Systematic Review of Prospective Studies.* 12(10) PLoS ONE. *See also* Christina Maslach & Michael Leiter (2016). *Understanding the Burnout Experience: Recent Research and Its Implications for Psychiatry.* 15(2) World Psychiatry 103–111.

26 Educating leaders about burnout is an important first step organizations should take when addressing this topic, and it's an important part of my work.

27 Mina Westman & Dalia Etzion (2001). *The Impact of Vacation and Job Stress and Burnout and Absenteeism.* 16(5) Psychology and Health 95–106.

28 Daniel S. Tawfik et al. (2018). *Physician Burnout, Well-Being, and Work Unit Safety Grades in Relationship to Reported Medical Errors.* 93(11) Mayo Clinical Proceedings 1–18.

29 For a summary of studies in healthcare, see Tait Shanafelt, Joel Goh, & Christine Sinsky (September 25, 2017). *The Business Case for Investing in Physician Well-Being.* JAMA Internal Medicine, Special Communication, E1–E7. *See also* Maryam S. Hamidi et al. (2018). *Estimating Institutional Physician Turnover Attributable to Self-Reported Burnout and Associated Financial Burden: A Case Study.* 18(1) BMC Health Services Research 851.

30 *Supra* note 18 Bakker, Demerouti, & Sanz-Vergel at 397.

31 Tait D. Shanafelt et al. (2016). *Longitudinal Study Evaluating the Association Between Physician Burnout and Changes in Professional Work Effort.* 91(4) Mayo Clinic Proceedings 422–431.

32 *Supra* note 2 at E3.

33 *Supra* note 29 Hamidi et al.

Chapter 2

1 Stephen Swensen, Andrea Kabcenell, & Tait Shanafelt (2016). *Physician-Organization Collaboration Reduces Physician Burnout and Promotes Engagement: The Mayo Clinic Experience.* 61(2) Journal of Healthcare Management 105–127.

2 Tait D. Shanafelt & John H. Noseworthy (2017). *Executive Leadership and Physician Well-Being: Nine Organizational Strategies to Promote Engagement and Reduce Burnout.* 92(1) Mayo Clinic Proceedings 129–146.

3 *Id.* at 142.

4 *Supra* note 1 at 105, 114.

5 *Id.* at 109.

6 Christina Maslach & Julie Goldberg (1998). *Prevention of Burnout: New Perspectives.* 7 Applied and Preventive Psychology 63–74.

7 Michael P. Leiter & Christina Maslach (January/February 2015). Conquering Burnout. *Scientific American Mind. See also* Pascale M. LeBlanc et al. (2007). *Take Care! The Evaluation of a Team-Based Burnout Prevention Intervention Program for Oncology Care Providers.* 92(1) Journal of Applied Psychology 213–227.

8 Maria Panagioti et al. (2017). *Controlled Interventions to Reduce Burnout in Physicians: A Systemic Review and Meta-Analysis.* 177(2) JAMA Internal Medicine 195–205.

9 Wendy L. Awa, Martina Plaumann, & Ulla Walter (2010). *Burnout Prevention: A Review of Intervention Programs.* 78 Patient Education and Counseling 184–190.

10 Kirsi Ahola, Salla Toppinen-Tanner, & Johanna Seppanen (2017). *Interventions to Alleviate Burnout Symptoms and to Support Return to Work Among Employees with Burnout: Systemic Review and Meta-Analysis.* 4 Burnout Research 1–11.

11 Tait Shanafelt, Joel Goh, & Christine Sinsky (September 25, 2017). *The Business Case for Investing in Physician Well-Being.* JAMA Internal Medicine, Special Communication, E1–E7.

12 Lizzy McLellan (February 19, 2020). Lawyers Reveal True Depth of Mental Health Struggles. Retrieved on February 19, 2020, at https://www.law.com/2020/02/19/lawyers-reveal-true-depth-of-the-mental-health-struggles.

13 *Id.*

14   Martin E. P. Seligman (2018). *The Hope Circuit* 326. New York: Public Affairs.
      The Master Resilience Trainer (MRT) program was developed based on a
      number of programs created and empirically validated by the University of
      Pennsylvania, including the Penn Resilience Program (PRP) and a parallel
      program called APEX; it incorporated a number of positive psychology
      concepts. The PRP has been evaluated in at least 19 controlled studies and,
      although some inconsistent findings have been reported, the studies suggest that
      PRP significantly reduces symptoms of depression and anxiety and helps
      participants perform better. More importantly, in the studies that included
      long-term follow-ups, PRP resilience skill effects were found to last for two years
      or more. In addition, the research on the PRP also demonstrated that teachers
      who are trained in the PRP can subsequently teach resilience skills effectively,
      lending support to the train-the-trainer model developed by Penn and
      incorporated in the MRT program. The research supporting these statements is
      as follows: Jane E. Gillham, Karen J. Reivich, & Lisa H. Jaycox (2008). *The Penn
      Resiliency Program* (also known as the Penn Depression Prevention Program
      and the Penn Optimism Program). Unpublished manuscript, University of
      Pennsylvania; Jane E. Gillam et al. (1991). The APEX Project: Manual for Group
      Leaders. Unpublished manuscript, University of Pennsylvania; *see also* Karen
      Reivich, Andrew Shatté, & Jane Gillham (2003). Penn Resilience Training for
      College Students: Leader's Guide and Participant's Guide. Unpublished
      manuscript, University of Pennsylvania; and Steven M. Brunwasser, Jane E.
      Gillham, & Eric S. Kim (2009). *A Meta-Analytic Review of the Penn Resiliency
      Program's Effects on Depressive Symptoms.* 77 Journal of Consulting and Clinical
      Psychology 1042–1054.

15   All the information in this paragraph, including the quote, comes from
      George W. Casey Jr. (2011). *Comprehensive Soldier Fitness: A Vision for
      Psychological Resilience in the U.S. Army.* 66(1) American Psychologist 1–3. Note
      that the program was initially called Comprehensive Soldier Fitness but changed
      its name to Comprehensive Soldier and Family Fitness as the program evolved
      to train spouses and family members.

16   You can read more about how the program was created here: Martin E. P.
      Seligman (2018). *The Hope Circuit* 311–327. New York: Public Affairs; *see also*
      Karen J. Reivich, Martin E. P. Seligman, & Sharon McBride (2011). *Master
      Resilience Training in the U.S. Army.* 66(1) American Psychologist 25–34; *also,*
      personal conversation with Lt. Col. Sylvia Lopez as to the current number of
      MRTs.

17   To learn more, you can visit the CSF2 page on the Army Resilience Directorate
      website at https://readyandresilient.army.mil/CSF2/index.html.

18   Paula Davis-Laack (2018). *From Army Strong to Lawyer Strong: What the Legal
      Profession Can Learn from the Army's Experience Cultivating a Culture of
      Resilience.* A self-published e-book.

19   Tait D. Shanafelt et al. (2015). *Impact of Organizational Leadership on Physician
      Burnout and Satisfaction.* 90(4) Mayo Clinic Proceedings 432–440.

20 *Supra* note 1 at 109. In addition, the components of the Listen-Act-Develop model have continued to be refined through various in-house studies and initiatives.

21 *Supra* note 14.

Chapter 3

1 Rachel L. Narel, Therese Yaeger, & Peter F. Sorensen Jr. (2019). Exploring Agile and Thriving Teams in Continuous Change Environments in *Research in Organizational Change and Development* (Abraham B. [Rami] Shani & Debra A. Noumair, eds.). Volume 27, 187–211. United Kingdom: Emerald.

2 Interview with Alyssa Brennan on March 25, 2020.

3 Lecture delivered by Prof. Scott A. Westfahl on March 9, 2020.

4 Kirsten Weir (2018). *What Makes Teams Work?* 49(8) Monitor on Psychology 46–54.

5 Amy C. Edmondson (2012). *Teaming: How Organizations Learn, Innovate, and Compete in the Knowledge Economy* 27. San Francisco: Jossey Bass.

6 For a summary of all the studies looking at the outcomes of high-performing teams and well-being, see Cynthia D. Smith et al. (2018). *Implementing Optimal Team-Based Care to Reduce Clinician Burnout.* Discussion Paper, National Academy of Medicine, Washington, DC.

7 Annalena Welp & Tanja Manser (2016). *Integrating Teamwork, Clinician Occupational Well-Being and Patient Safety—Development of a Conceptual Framework Based on a Systematic Review.* 16(1) BMC Health Services Research 281.

8 Rachel Willard-Grace et al. (2014). *Team Structure and Culture Are Associated with Lower Burnout in Primary Care.* 27(2) Journal of the American Board of Family Medicine 229–238. Richard W. Dehn et al. (2015). *Commentaries on Health Services Research.* 28(6) Journal of the American Board of Family Medicine 1–3.

9 Arla L. Day et al. (2009). *Workplace Risks and Stressors as Predictors of Burnout: The Moderating Impact of Job Control and Team Efficacy.* 26 Canadian Journal of Administrative Sciences 7–22.

10 Stefan Razinskas & Martin Hoegl (2020). *A Multilevel Review of Stressor Research in Teams.* 41 Journal of Organizational Behavior 185–209.

11 *Id.* at 196.

12 Dragan Mijakoski et al. (2015). *Differences in Burnout, Work Demands and Team Work Between Croatian and Macedonian Hospital Nurses.* 19(3) Cognition, Brain, Behavior. An Interdisciplinary Journal 179–200.

13 Somava Stout et al. (2017). *Developing High-Functioning Teams: Factors Associated with Operating as a "Real Team" and Implications for Patient-Centered Medical Home Development.* 54 Journal of Health Care, Organization, Provision and Financing 1–9.

14   Pascale M. LeBlanc et al. (2007). *Take Care! The Evaluation of a Team-Based Burnout Intervention Program for Oncology Care Providers.* 92(1) Journal of Applied Psychology 213–227.

15   David M. Fisher, Jennifer M. Ragsdale, & Emily C. S. Fisher (2019). *The Importance of Definitional and Temporal Issues in the Study of Resilience.* 68(4) Applied Psychology: An International Review 583–620.

16   *Id.*

17   George M. Alliger, Christopher P. Cerasoli, Scott I. Tannenbaum, & William B. Vessey (2015). *Team Resilience: How Teams Flourish Under Pressure.* 44 Organizational Dynamics 176–184.

18   Christine Porath, Gretchen Spreitzer, Cristina Gibson, & Flannery G. Garnett (2012). *Thriving at Work: Toward Its Measurement, Construct Validation, and Theoretical Refinement.* 33 Journal of Organizational Behavior 250–275.

19   *Supra* note 1 at 188.

20   *Id.* at 194.

21   *Id.* at 204.

22   Anne-Kathrin Kleine, Cort W. Randolph, & Hannes Zacher (2019). *Thriving at Work: A Meta-Analysis.* 40 Journal of Organizational Behavior 973–999, showing a strong negative correlation of −.53.

23   *Supra* note 18 at 250–251, 263.

24   This list is from my own work in combination with the following resources: Paul B. C. Morgan, David Fletcher, & Mustafa Sarkar (2019). *Developing Team Resilience: A Season-Long Study of Psychosocial Enablers and Strategies in a High-Level Sports Team.* 45 Psychology of Sport & Exercise 1–11; Patricia Lopes Costa et al. (2017). *Interactions in Engaged Work Teams: A Qualitative Study.* 23(5/6) Team Performance Management: An International Journal 206–226; Christina N. Lacerenza, Shannon L. Marlow, Scott I. Tannenbaum, & Eduardo Salas (2018). *Team Development Interventions: Evidence-Based Approaches for Improving Teamwork.* 73(4) American Psychologist 517–531; Eduardo Salas, Stephanie Zajac, & Shannon L. Marlow (2018). *Transforming Health Care One Team at a Time: Ten Observations and the Trail Ahead.* 43(3) Group & Organizational Management 357–381; Lea Waters et al. (2020). *Does Team Psychological Capital Predict Team Outcomes at Work?* 10(1) International Journal of Wellbeing 1–25; Isabella Meneghel, Isabel M. Martinez, & Marisa Salanova (2016). *Job-Related Antecedents of Team Resilience and Improved Team Performance.* 45(3) Personnel Review 505–522; Patricia Costa, Ana Margarida Passos, & Arnold Bakker (2014). *Empirical Validation of the Team Work Engagement Construct.* 13(1) Journal of Personnel Psychology 34–45; Bradley J. West, Jaime L. Patera, & Melissa K. Carsten (2009). *Team Level Positivity: Investigating Positive Psychological Capacities and Team Level Outcomes.* 30 Journal of Organizational Behavior 249–267; Janet McCray, Adam Palmer, & Nik Chmiel (2016). *Building Resilience in Health and*

Social Care Teams. 45(6) Personnel Review 1132–1155; Perry E. Geue (2017). *Positive Practices in the Workplace: Impact on Team Climate, Work Engagement and Task Performance*. 10(1) Emerging Leadership Journeys 70–99.

25 Stefan Razinskas & Martin Hoegl (2020). *A Multilevel Review of Stressor Research in Teams*. 41 Journal of Organizational Behavior 185–209.

26 *Supra* note 4 at 49–50.

Chapter 4

1 M. Lance Frazier et al. (2017). *Psychological Safety: A Meta-Analytic Review and Extension*. 70(1) Personnel Psychology 113–165.

2 *Id.*

3 Charles Duhigg (February 25, 2016). What Google Learned from Its Quest to Build the Perfect Team. *New York Times*. Retrieved on May 9, 2020, at https://www.nytimes.com/2016/02/28/magazine/what-google-learned-from-its-quest-to-build-the-perfect-team.html.

4 Email correspondence with Mary Shen O'Carroll on June 1, 2020.

5 Ingrid M. Nembhard & Amy C. Edmondson (2012). Psychological Safety: Foundations for Speaking Up, Collaboration, and Experimentation in Organizations in *The Oxford Handbook of Positive Organizational Scholarship* (Kim S. Cameron and Gretchen M. Spreitzer, eds.) 490–503. New York: Oxford University Press. *See also* Amy C. Edmondson (2012). *Teaming: How Organizations Learn, Innovate, and Compete in the Knowledge Economy* 139. San Francisco: Jossey-Bass. Amy C. Edmondson (2018). *The Fearless Organization: Creating Psychological Safety in the Workplace for Learning, Innovation, and Growth* 159. Hoboken, NJ: John Wiley & Sons. George M. Alliger, Christopher P. Cerasoli, Scott I. Tannenbaum, & William B. Vessey (2015). *Team Resilience: How Teams Flourish Under Pressure*. 44 Organizational Dynamics 176–184.

6 Abraham Carmeli, Daphna Brueller, & Jane Dutton (2009). *Learning Behaviours in the Workplace: The Role of High-Quality Interpersonal Relationships and Psychological Safety*. 26 Systems Research and Behavioral Science 81–98. *See also Id.* at 498.

7 Edward L. Deci & Richard M. Ryan (2014). The Importance of Universal Psychological Needs for Understanding Motivation in the Workplace in *The Oxford Handbook of Work Engagement, Motivation, and Self-Determination Theory* (Marylène Gagné, ed.) 13–32. New York: Oxford University Press.

8 Edward L. Deci & Richard M. Ryan (2000). *The "What" and "Why" of Goal Pursuits: Human Needs and the Self-Determination of Behavior*. 11(4) Psychological Inquiry 227–268. *See also* Maarten Vansteenkiste, Richard M. Ryan, & Bart Soenens (2020). *Basic Psychological Need Theory: Advancements, Critical Themes, and Future Directions*. 44 Motivation and Emotions 1–31.

9 Donald K. Freeborn (2001). *Satisfaction, Commitment, and Psychological Well-Being Among HMO Physicians*. 174(1) Western Journal of Medicine 13–18.

10   Adapted from Jessica Perlo et al. (2017). *IHI Framework for Improving Joy in Work.* 18 IHI White Paper. Cambridge, MA: Institute for Healthcare Improvement.

11   Marylène Gagné & Maarten Vansteenkiste (2013). Self-Determination Theory's Contribution to Positive Organizational Psychology in *Advances in Positive Organizational Psychology* (Arnold B. Bakker, ed.) 61–82. United Kingdom: Emerald.

12   Claude Fernet, Stéphanie Austin, Sarah-Geneviève Trépanier, & Marc Dussault (2013). *How Do Job Characteristics Contribute to Burnout? Exploring the Distinct Mediating Roles of Perceived Autonomy, Competence, & Relatedness.* 22(2) European Journal of Work and Organizational Psychology 123–137. *See also* Anja Van den Broeck, Maarten Vansteenkiste, Hans De Witte, & Willy Lens (2008). *Explaining the Relationships Between Job Characteristics, Burnout, and Engagement: The Role of Basic Psychological Need Satisfaction.* 22(3) Work & Stress 277–294.

13   Anja Van den Broeck, D. Lance Ferris, Chu-Hsiang Chang, & Christopher C. Rosen (2016). *A Review of Self-Determination Theory's Basic Psychological Needs at Work.* 42(5) Journal of Management 1195–1229.

14   Peter Rouse et al. (2020). *The Interplay Between Psychological Need Satisfaction and Psychological Need Frustration Within a Work Context: A Variable and Person-Oriented Approach.* 44 Motivation and Emotion 175–189.

15   *Supra* note 11 at 69. *See also* Reed W. Larson, Carolyn Orson, & Jill R. Bowers (2017). Positive Youth Development: How Intrinsic Motivation Amplifies Adolescents' Social-Emotional Learning in *Scientific Advances in Positive Psychology* (Meg A. Warren and Stewart I. Donaldson, eds.) 165–194. Santa Barbara, CA: Praeger.

16   Gretchen M. Spreitzer & Christine Porath (2014). Self-Determination as a Nutriment for Thriving: Building an Integrative Model of Human Growth at Work in *The Oxford Handbook of Work Engagement, Motivation, and Self-Determination* (Marylène Gagné, ed.) 245–258. New York: Oxford University Press. *See also* Gretchen M. Spreitzer & Christine Porath (2014). Enabling Thriving at Work in *How to Be a Positive Leader* (Jane E. Dutton and Gretchen M. Spreitzer, eds.) 45–54. San Francisco: Berrett-Koehler.

17   Bruce Tulgan (1999). *FAST Feedback*, 2nd ed. Amherst, MA: HRD.

Chapter 5

1   Nicholas Epley & Juliana Schroeder (2014). *Mistakenly Seeking Solitude.* 143(5) Journal of Experimental Psychology: General 1980–1999.

2   Roy F. Baumeister & Mark R. Leary (1995). *The Need to Belong: Desire for Interpersonal Attachments as a Fundamental Human Motivation.* 117(3) Psychological Bulletin 497–529. *See also* Edward L. Deci & Richard M. Ryan (2000). *The "What" and "Why" of Goal Pursuits: Human Needs and the Self-Determination of Behavior.* 11 Psychological Inquiry 227–268.

3 Claude Fernet, Olivier Torres, Stéphanie Austin, & Josée St-Pierre (2016). *The Psychological Costs of Owning and Managing and SME: Linking Job Stressors, Occupational Loneliness, Entrepreneurial Orientation, and Burnout.* 3 Burnout Research 45–53. *See also* Eamonn Rogers, Andrea N. Polonijo, & Richard M. Carpiano (2016). *Getting By with a Little Help from Friends and Colleagues: Testing How Residents' Social Support Networks Affect Loneliness and Burnout.* 62 Canadian Family Physician 677–683; Emma Seppala and Marissa King (June 29, 2017). Burnout at Work Isn't Just About Exhaustion: It's Also About Loneliness. *Harvard Business Review.* Retrieved on May 17, 2020, at https://hbr .org/2017/06/burnout-at-work-isnt-just-about-exhaustion-its-also-about -loneliness.

4 Wendell David Cockshaw, Ian M. Shochet, & Patricia L. Obst (2014). *Depression and Belongingness in General and Workplace Contexts: A Cross-Lagged Longitudinal Investigation.* 33(5) Journal of Social and Clinical Psychology 448–462.

5 Shawn Achor, Gabriella Rosen Kellerman, Andrew Reece, & Alexi Robichaux (March 19, 2018). America's Loneliest Workers, According to Research. *Harvard Business Review.* Retrieved on May 20, 2020, at https://hbr.org/2018/03/americas -loneliest-workers-according-to-research.

6 Hakan Ozcelik & Sigal Barsade (2011). *Work Loneliness and Employee Performance.* 1 Academy of Management Proceedings.

7 *Id.*

8 John T. Cacioppo & William Patrick (2008). *Loneliness* 228–244. New York: Norton.

9 Claude Fernet, Stéphanie Austin, Sarah-Geneviève Trépanier, & Marc Dussault (2013). *How Do Job Characteristics Contribute to Burnout? Exploring the Distinct Mediating Roles of Perceived Autonomy, Competence, & Relatedness.* 22(2) European Journal of Work and Organizational Psychology 123–137.

10 Ingrid M. Nembhard & Amy C. Edmondson (2012). Psychological Safety: Foundations for Speaking Up, Collaboration, and Experimentation in Organizations in *The Oxford Handbook of Positive Organizational Scholarship* (Kim S. Cameron and Gretchen M. Spreitzer, eds.) 490–503. New York: Oxford University Press.

11 Mark Mortensen (2015). Leading Teams of Lawyers in an Increasingly Global and Virtual World in *Leadership for Lawyers* (Rebecca Normand-Hochman & Heidi K. Gardner, eds.) 35–47. London: Global Law and Business. *See also* Ana-Cristina Costa, C. A. Fulmer, & Neil Anderson (2018). *Trust in Work Teams: An Integrative Review, Multilevel Model, and Future Directions.* 39(2) Journal of Organizational Behavior 169–184.

12 Harry T. Reis et al. (2010). *Are You Happy for Me? How Sharing Positive Events with Others Provides Personal and Interpersonal Benefits.* 99(2) Journal of Personality and Social Psychology 311–329.

13 *Id.* at 321–322.

14   Shelly L. Gable & Harry T. Reis (2010). *Good News! Capitalizing on Positive Events in an Interpersonal Context.* 42 Advances in Experimental Social Psychology 195–257. *See also* Shelly L. Gable, Gian C. Gonzaga, & Amy Strachman (2006). *Will You Be There for Me When Things Go Right? Supportive Responses to Positive Event Disclosures.* 91(5) Journal of Personality and Social Psychology 904–917. Shelly L. Gable & Courtney L. Gosnell (2011). The Positive Side of Close Relationships in *Designing Positive Psychology* (Kennon M. Sheldon, Todd B. Kashdan, & Michael F. Steger, eds.) 265–279. New York: Oxford University Press.

15   This is a combination of roadblocks I was taught at the University of Pennsylvania along with others I've been asked about during my workshops.

16   The phrases "Joy Multiplier" and "Joy Thief" were created by Dr. Karen Reivich and used as part of the University of Pennsylvania team's instruction of this skill to US Army personnel as part of the US Army's Comprehensive Soldier and Family Fitness program.

17   Jingqiu Chen, Peter A. Bamberger, Yifan Song, & Dana R. Vashdi (2018). *The Effects of Team Reflexivity on Psychological Well-Being in Manufacturing Teams.* 103(4) Journal of Applied Psychology 443–462. *See also* Christina N. Lacerenza, Shannon L. Marlow, Scott I. Tannenbaum, & Eduardo Salas (2018). *Team Development Interventions: Evidence-Based Approaches for Improving Teamwork.* 73(4) American Psychologist 517–531.

18   *Id.* Chen et al. at 455–456.

19   Anton J. Villado & Winfred Arthur Jr. (2013). *The Comparative Effect of Subjective and Objective After-Action Reviews on Team Performance on a Complex Task.* 98(3) Journal of Applied Psychology 514–528.

20   I first learned a version of this communication model during my work with US Army drill sergeants at the University of Pennsylvania. The basis of that model comes from Sharon Anthony Bower & Gordon H. Bower (2004). *Asserting Yourself: A Practical Guide for Positive Change.* New York: De Capo Press.

Chapter 6

1   Michael F. Steger & Bryan J. Dik (2010). Work as Meaning: Individual and Organizational Benefits of Engaging in Meaningful Work in *Oxford Handbook of Positive Psychology and Work* (P. Alex Linley, Susan Harrington, & Nicola Garcea, eds.) 131–142. New York: Oxford University Press.

2   Blake A. Allan, Ryan D. Duffy, & Brian Collisson (2018). *Helping Others Increases Meaningful Work: Evidence from Three Experiments.* 65(2) Journal of Counseling Psychology 155–165.

3   *Id.*

4   Dariusz Krok (2016). *Can Meaning Buffer Work Pressure? An Exploratory Study on Styles of Meaning in Life and Burnout in Firefighters.* 1 Archives of Psychiatry and Psychotherapy 31–42.

5   *Supra* note 2. And for those of you who are science geeks, the correlation between meaningful work and intrinsic types of motivation is .83!

6   Marylène Gagné et al. (2015). *The Multidimensional Work Motivation Scale: Validation Evidence in Seven Languages and Nine Countries.* 24(2) European Journal of Work and Organizational Psychology 178–196.

7   C. Scott Rigby & Richard M. Ryan (2018). *Self-Determination Theory in Human Resource Development: New Directions and Practical Considerations.* 20(2) Advances in Developing Human Resources 133–147.

8   Gavin R. Slemp, Margaret L. Kern, Kent J. Patrick, & Richard M. Ryan (2018). *Leader Autonomy Support in the Workplace: A Meta-Analytic Review.* 42 Motivation and Emotion 706–724.

9   Yu-Lan Su & Johnmarshall Reeve (2011). *A Meta-Analysis of the Effectiveness of Intervention Programs Designed to Support Autonomy.* 23 Educational Psychology Review 159–188. *See also* Johnmarshall Reeve (2015). *Giving and Summoning Autonomy Support in Hierarchical Relationships.* 9(8) Social and Personality Psychology Compass 406–418. Patricia L. Hardre & Johnmarshall Reeve (2009). *Training Corporate Managers to Adopt a More Autonomy-Supportive Motivating Style Toward Employees: An Intervention Study.* 13(3) International Journal of Training and Development 165–184.

10 *Supra* note 8. *See also* Dan N. Stone, Edward L. Deci, & Richard M. Ryan (2009). *Beyond Talk: Creating Autonomous Motivation Through Self-Determination Theory.* 34(3) Journal of General Management 75–91.

11 Marcia Reynolds (2020). *Coach the Person Not the Problem: A Guide to Using Reflective Inquiry* 113. San Francisco: Berrett-Koehler.

12 Tait D. Shanafelt et al. (2009). *Career Fit and Burnout Among Academic Faculty.* 169(10) JAMA Internal Medicine 990–995.

13 Rob Baker (2020). *Personalization at Work: How HR Can Use Job Crafting to Drive Performance, Engagement and Wellbeing* 145. New York: Kogen Page.

14 Frank Martela, Richard M. Ryan, & Michael F. Steger (2018). *Meaningfulness as Satisfaction of Autonomy, Competence, Relatedness, and Beneficence: Comparing the Four Satisfactions and Positive Affect as Predictors of Meaning in Life.* 19 Journal of Happiness Studies 1261–1282.

15 *Supra* note 2.

16 Telephone interview with Harvard Business School Professor Jon Jachimowicz, who was part of the research team that worked with these nurses, May 28, 2020. *See also* Darshan Patel (March 22, 2018). *It's Not All About Pay: Helping Nurses Sustain Their Passion Through Timely Feedback.* Retrieved on June 4, 2020, at https://www.health.org.uk/blogs/it's-not-all-about-pay-helping-nurses-sustain -their-passion-through-timely-feedback.

17 Adam M. Grant et al. (2007). *Impact and the Art of Motivation Maintenance: The Effects of Contact with Beneficiaries on Persistence Behavior.* 103(1) Organizational Behavior and Human Decision Processes 53–67.

18 Yehonatan Turner, Shuli Silberman, Sandor Joffe, & Irith Hadas-Halpern (2008). *The Effect of Adding a Patient's Photograph to the Radiographic Examination.* Annual Meeting of the Radiological Society of North America. *See also* Adam Grant (2013). *Give and Take* 166. New York: Viking.

19 Adam M. Grant (2014). Outsource Inspiration in *How to Be a Positive Leader* (Jane E. Dutton and Gretchen M. Spreitzer, eds.) 22–31. San Francisco: Berrett-Koehler.

20 Dr. Kelly McGonigal writes about bigger-than-self goals in her wonderful book, *The Upside of Stress* (2015) 143–151. New York: Avery.

Chapter 7

1 Alia J. Crum, William R. Corbin, Kelly D. Brownell, & Peter Salovey (2011). *Mind over Milkshakes: Mindsets, Not Just Nutrients, Determine Ghrelin Response.* 30(4) Health Psychology 424–429.

2 Alia J. Crum, Peter Salovey, & Shawn Achor (2013). *Rethinking Stress: The Role of Mindsets in Determining the Stress Response.* 104(4) Journal of Personality and Social Psychology 716–733.

3 Gerald F. Goodwin, Nikki Blacksmith, & Meredith R. Coats (2018). *The Science of Teams in the Military: Contributions from Over 60 Years of Research.* 73(4) American Psychologist 322–333.

4 Although I will mention certain studies specifically, the work in this section stems largely from Dr. Albert Bandura. To learn more about the types and nuances of efficacy, please read Albert Bandura (1997). *The Exercise of Control.* New York: Freeman.

5 Kotaro Shoji et al. (2015). *Associations Between Job Burnout and Self-Efficacy: A Meta-Analysis.* 29(4) Anxiety, Stress, & Coping 367–386. *See also* Mercedes Ventura, Marisa Salanova, & Susan Llorens (2015). *Professional Self-Efficacy as a Predictor of Burnout and Engagement: The Role of Challenge and Hindrance Demands.* 149(3) Journal of Psychology 277–302.

6 Albert Bandura (2000). *Exercise of Human Agency Through Collective Efficacy.* 9(3) Current Directions in Psychological Science 75–78.

7 *Id.* at 76. *See also* Bradley J. West, Jaime L. Patera, & Melissa K. Carsten (2009). *Team Level Positivity: Investigating Positive Psychological Capacities and Team Level Outcomes.* Maria Vera, Alma M. Rodriguez-Sanchez, & Marisa Salanova (2017). *May the Force Be with You: Looking for Resources That Build Team Resilience.* 32(2) Journal of Workplace Behavioral Health 119–138.

8 Arla L. Day et al. (2009). *Workplace Risks and Stressors as Predictors of Burnout: The Moderating Impact of Job Control and Team Efficacy.* 26 Canadian Journal of Administrative Sciences 7–22.

9 Paul B. C. Morgan, David Fletcher, & Mustafa Sarkar (2013). *Defining and Characterizing Team Resilience in Elite Sport.* 14 Psychology of Sport and Exercise 549–559.

10 *Supra* note 6. *See also* Daniel F. Gucciardi et al. (2018). *The Emergence of Team Resilience: A Multilevel Conceptual Model of Facilitating Factors*. 91 Journal of Occupational and Organizational Psychology 729–768. Roger D. Goddard & Serena J. Salloum (2012). Collective Efficacy Beliefs, Organizational Excellence, & Leadership in *The Oxford Handbook of Positive Organizational Scholarship* (Kim S. Cameron & Gretchen M. Spreitzer, eds.) 642–650. New York: Oxford University Press.

11 Albert Bandura (2009). Cultivate Self-Efficacy for Personal and Organizational Effectiveness in *Handbook of Principles of Organizational Behavior*, 2nd ed. (Edwin A. Locke, ed.) 179–200. UK: John Wiley & Sons.

12 I first learned about these triggers from Dr. Karen Reivich, both in my applied positive psychology program at the University of Pennsylvania and later in my US Army resilience training work.

13 S. Joyce et al. (2016). *Workplace Interventions for Common Mental Disorders: A Systematic Meta-Review*. 46 Psychological Medicine 683–697. *See also* Karen Reivich, Martin E. P. Seligman, & Sharon McBride (2011). *Master Resilience Training in the U.S. Army*. 66(1) American Psychologist 25–34.

14 I drew on ideas and concepts for this model from the work of Drs. Martin E. P. Seligman, Judith S. Beck, and Alia Crum. In particular, see So-Hyeon Shim, Alia J. Crum, & Adam Galinsky. The Grace of Control: How a Can-Control Mindset Increases Well-Being, Health & Performance. 2016 *in submission*.

15 The research efficacy and ideas in this section are explained in Judith S. Beck (2011). *Cognitive Behavior Therapy Basics & Beyond*, 2nd ed., 172. New York: Guilford Press; and in Karen Reivich & Andrew Shatté (2002). *The Resilience Factor* 168–185. New York: Broadway Books. The foundation of this work derives from Dr. Albert Ellis and Dr. Aaron T. Beck.

Chapter 8

1 Telephone conversation with Dr. Michele ("Micki") Fagan on May 27, 2020, and subsequent email exchanges thereafter, specifically June 24, 2020.

2 Telephone conversation with Dr. Christine Rizkalla on September 15, 2020.

3 Tait D. Shanafelt et al. (2020). *Association of Burnout, Professional Fulfillment, and Self-Care Practices of Physician Leaders with Their Independently Rated Leadership Effectiveness*. 3(6) JAMA Network Open. https://doi.org/10.1001/jamanetworkopen.2020.7961.

4 Tait D. Shanafelt et al. (2015). *Impact of Organizational Leadership on Physician Burnout & Satisfaction*. 90(4) Mayo Clinic Proceedings 432–440.

5 Paula Davis-Laack & Scott Westfahl (June 15, 2019). Five Things That Resilient Teams Do Differently. *Fast Company*. https://www.fastcompany.com/90364553/5-things-that-resilient-teams-do-differently.

6 Heidi K. Gardner (July 20, 2015). Juggling the Producer-Manager Roles. *Professional Collaborations* blog. Retrieved on November 22, 2020, at https://

professionalcollaborations.wordpress.com/2015/07/20/juggling-the-producer
-manager-roles/.

7   Arnold B. Bakker, Hetty van Emmerik, & Martin D. Euwema (2006). *Crossover of Burnout and Engagement in Work Teams*. 33(4) Work and Occupation 464–489.

8   Emily D. Dolan et al. (2014). *Using a Single Item to Measure Burnout in Primary Care Staff: A Psychometric Evaluation*. 30(5) Journal of General Internal Medicine 582–587.

9   Sigal G. Barsade (2002). *The Ripple Effect: Emotional Contagion and Its Influence on Group Behavior*. 47 Administrative Science Quarterly 644–675.

10 Roy F. Baumeister, Ellen Bratslavsky, Catrin Finkenauer, & Kathleen D. Vohs (2001). *Bad Is Stronger Than Good*. 5(4) Review of General Psychology 323–370.

11 Ed Diener, Stuti Thapa, & Louis Tay (2020). *Positive Emotions at Work*. 7 Annual Review of Organizational Psychology and Organizational Behavior 451–477. For a great overview of positive emotions generally, see Barbara L. Fredrickson (2013). *Positive Emotions Broaden and Build*. 47 Advances in Experimental Social Psychology 1–53.

12 Isabella Meneghel, Marisa Salanova, & Isabel M. Martinez (2016). *Feeling Good Makes Us Stronger: How Team Resilience Mediates the Effect of Positive Emotions on Team Performance*. 17 Journal of Happiness Studies 239–255.

13 The ideas in this section come from the work of Teresa M. Amabile, Steven J. Kramer and their colleagues. I used the following resources: Teresa M. Amabile & Steven J. Kramer (May 2011). The Power of Small Wins. *Harvard Business Review*. Teresa Amabile & Steven Kramer (2011). *The Progress Principle: Using Small Wins to Ignite Joy, Engagement, and Creativity at Work*. Boston: Harvard Business Review Press.

14 The information in this section about icebergs comes from Karen Reivich & Andrew Shatté (2002). *The Resilience Factor* 123–144. New York: Broadway Books.

15 These themes appear over and over in my workshops and coaching conversations, but I appreciated how these themes were distilled in the following article: Dimitrios Tsatiris (November 29, 2020). 5 Anxiety-Provoking Habits Among High Achievers. *Psychology Today*. https://www.psychologytoday.com /us/blog/anxiety-in-high-achievers/202011/5-anxiety-provoking-habits-among -high-achievers.

Chapter 9

1   Ben J. Searle (2017). How Work Design Can Enhance or Erode Employee Resilience in *Managing For Resilience* (Monique F. Crane, ed.) 103–116. New York: Routledge. *See also* Marylène Gagné & Alexandra Panaccio (2014). The Motivational Power of Job Design in *The Oxford Handbook of Work Engagement, Motivation, and Self-Determination Theory* (Marylène Gagné, ed.) 165–180. New York: Oxford University Press.

2   Maria Tims & Arnold B. Bakker (2014). Job Design and Employee Engagement in *Employee Engagement in Theory and Practice* (Catherine Truss, Rick Delbridge, Kerstin Alfes, Amanda Shantz, & Emma Soane, eds.) 131–148. New York: Routledge.

3   Tino Lesener, Burkhard Gusy, Anna Jochmann, & Christine Wolter (2020). *The Drivers of Work Engagement: A Meta-Analytic Review of Longitudinal Evidence.* 34(3) Work & Stress 259–278.

4   George M. Alliger, Christopher P. Cerasoli, Scott I. Tannenbaum, & William B. Vessey (2015). *Team Resilience: How Teams Flourish Under Pressure.* 44 Organizational Dynamics 176–184.

5   Marshall Ganz has developed an entire method around using stories to leverage change called "public narrative." This is a good resource from Harvard University to learn more: https://dash.harvard.edu/bitstream/handle/1/30760283/Public-Narrative-Worksheet-Fall-2013.pdf.

6   Arnold B. Bakker et al. (2007). *Job Resources Boost Work Engagement, Particularly When Job Demands Are High.* 99 Journal of Educational Psychology 274–284.

7   Judith S. Beck (2011). *Cognitive Behavioral Therapy: The Basics and Beyond,* 2nd ed. New York: Guilford Press. Dr. Karen Reivich also included a version of these questions for a *Health* magazine article.

8   There are a number of strengths assessments, but my favorite is the Values in Action (VIA) Character Strengths Assessment. You can download it for free at https://www.viacharacter.org.

9   David L. Cooperrider, Diana Whitney, & Jacqueline M. Stavros (2008). *Appreciative Inquiry Handbook for Leaders of Change,* 2nd ed. Brunswick, OH: Crown Custom.

10 *Id.* at 177.

11 Adapted from Michelle McQuaid (2020). *Can A Question Change Your Life? The Art of Appreciative Inquiry.* The Change Lab.

12 Bill Burnett & Dave Evans (2017). *Designing Your Life: How to Build a Well-Lived, Joyful Life.* New York: Knopf. To learn more about how I applied design thinking principles and mindsets to change my career after I stopped practicing law, see Paula Davis-Laack (October 16, 2017). I Used Design Thinking to Reinvent My Career—Here Is Why It Worked. *Fast Company.* Retrieved on July 3, 2020, at https://www.fastcompany.com/40481175/i-used-design-thinking-to-reinvent-my-career-heres-why-it-worked.

13 The Stanford d.school has a short two-page lesson plan you can download here: https://dschool.stanford.edu/resources/spaghetti-marshmallow-challenge. *See also* this TED Talk by Tom Wujec about the history of the spaghetti challenge, which was first introduced by Peter Skillman: https://www.ted.com/talks/tom_wujec_build_a_tower_build_a_team/transcript?language=en.

14   The phrase "humble curiosity" originated with my friend and colleague, Caitlin "Cat" Moon.

15   Todd B. Kashdan, Ryne A. Sherman, Jessica Yarbro, & David C. Funder (2013). *How Are Curious People Viewed and How Do They Behave in Social Situations? From the Perspectives of Self, Friends, Parents, and Unacquainted Observers.* 81(2) Journal of Personality 142–154.

16   Edward L. Deci & Richard M. Ryan (2014). The Importance of Universal Psychological Needs for Understanding Motivation in the Workplace in *The Oxford Handbook of Work Engagement, Motivation, and Self-Determination Theory* (Marylène Gagné, ed.) 13–32. New York: Oxford University Press. *See also* Gavin R. Slemp, Margaret L. Kern, Kent J. Patrick, & Richard M. Ryan (2018). *Leader Autonomy Support in the Workplace: A Meta-Analytic Review.* 42 Motivation and Emotion 706–724.

Index

About the Author

Paula Davis, JD, MAPP, is the founder and CEO of the Stress & Resilience Institute, a training and consulting firm that partners with leaders and organizations to help them reduce burnout and build resilience at the team, leader, and organizational levels.

Paula left her law practice after seven years and earned a master's degree in applied positive psychology from the University of Pennsylvania. As part of her postgraduate training, Paula was selected to be part of the University of Pennsylvania faculty, teaching resilience skills to soldiers as part of the US Army's Comprehensive Soldier and Family Fitness program. The Penn team trained resilience skills to more than 40,000 soldiers and their family members.

Her expertise has been featured in the *New York Times*; *O, The Oprah Magazine*; the *Washington Post*; and many other publications. Paula is also a contributor to *Forbes, Fast Company,* and *Psychology Today.*

Paula is a two-time recipient of the distinguished teaching award from the Medical College of Wisconsin.

You can learn more about her work and get additional burnout prevention and resilience resources by visiting her website at www.stressandresilience.com. You can contact her directly at paula@stressandresilience.com.

WHARTON
SCHOOL
PRESS

About Wharton School Press

Wharton School Press, the book publishing arm of the Wharton School of the University of Pennsylvania, was established to inspire bold, insightful thinking within the global business community.

Wharton School Press publishes a select list of award-winning, best-selling, and thought-leading books that offer trusted business knowledge to help leaders at all levels meet the challenges of today and the opportunities of tomorrow. Led by a spirit of innovation and experimentation, Wharton School Press leverages groundbreaking digital technologies and has pioneered a fast-reading business book format that fits readers' busy lives, allowing them to swiftly emerge with the tools and information needed to make an impact. Wharton School Press books offer guidance and inspiration on a variety of topics, including leadership, management, strategy, innovation, entrepreneurship, finance, marketing, social impact, public policy, and more.

Wharton School Press also operates an online bookstore featuring a curated selection of influential books by Wharton School faculty and Press authors published by a wide range of leading publishers.

To find books that will inspire and empower you to increase your impact and expand your personal and professional horizons, visit *wsp.wharton.upenn.edu.*

UNIVERSITY of PENNSYLVANIA

About the Wharton School

Founded in 1881 as the world's first collegiate business school, the Wharton School of the University of Pennsylvania is shaping the future of business by incubating ideas, driving insights, and creating leaders who change the world. With a faculty of more than 235 renowned professors, Wharton has 5,000 undergraduate, MBA, executive MBA, and doctoral students. Each year 18,000 professionals from around the world advance their careers through Wharton Executive Education's individual, company-customized, and online programs. More than 99,000 Wharton alumni form a powerful global network of leaders who transform business every day.

www.wharton.upenn.edu

CPSIA information can be obtained
at www.ICGtesting.com
Printed in the USA
JSHW080039090323
38691JS00003B/4